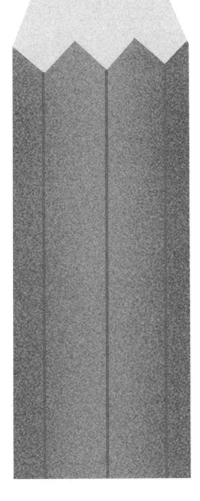

UP

FROM
UNDERACHIEVEMENT

How Teachers, Students, and Parents Can Work Together to Promote Student Success

DIANE HEACOX, Ed.D.

EDITED BY PAMELA ESPELAND

free spirit

Works for kids®

PUBLISHING®

Library of Congress Cataloging-in-Publication Data
Heacox, Diane. 1949–
 Up from underachievement : how teachers, students, and parents can work together to promote student success / by Diane Heacox ; edited by Pamela Espeland.
  p.   cm.
 Includes index.
 ISBN 0-915793-35-0
 1. Underachievers—United States. 2. Motivation in education.
 I. Espeland, Pamela, 1951– . II. Title
 LC4691.H43 1991   91-19069
 371.9—dc 20   CIP

The following are registered trademarks of Free Spirit Publishing Inc.:

FREE SPIRIT®
FREE SPIRIT PUBLISHING®
SELF-HELP FOR TEENS®
SELF-HELP FOR KIDS®
WORKS FOR KIDS®
THE FREE SPIRITED CLASSROOM®

free spirit
PUBLiSHiNG®
Works
for kids®

20 19 18 17 16 15 14 13 12 11 10 9
Printed in Canada

Cover design by Dao Nguyen
Book design by MacLean & Tuminelly

Free Spirit Publishing Inc.
400 First Avenue North, Suite 616
Minneapolis, MN 55401-1724
(612) 338-2068
help4kids@freespirit.com
www.freespirit.com

The health-related characteristics listed on pages 100–101 are adapted from Lawrence J. Greene, *Kids Who Underachieve* (New York: Simon and Schuster, 1986), pp. 252–254. Used with permission of Lawrence J. Greene.

DEDICATION

To my husband, John Bloodsworth, whose love, encouragement to grow, and unconditional support have sustained me.

To Kylie, for the extraordinary opportunity to be your mommy.

To my parents, who have always had the faith in me to be what I needed to be.

ACKNOWLEDGMENTS

I wish to thank my publisher, Judy Galbraith, for her faith in me. She gave me the creative freedom to write a book we both hope will help the kids we care so deeply about.

My thanks also go to Pamela Espeland, an editor who understands, respects, and refines an author's words. Her personal support and enthusiasm for this book have been important to me.

Finally, and especially, I need to thank the students I have known over my nineteen years in education. Knowing you, caring about you, and wanting to make school a better place for you have led to the strategies presented in this book. To those of you who are now adults, I hope you are continuing to live happy and satisfying lives. To those of you I am still working with, I need to say, "We won't give up."

CONTENTS

Introduction 1
A Widespread Problem 2
Jim's Story...2
Who Is Responsible? 3
Partnerships for Positive Change 3
How Long Will It Take for Change? 4

How to Use This Book 6
If a Student Is Currently Succeeding in School.................6
If a Student Is Underachieving in School..........................7

THE PLAYERS 9
Eight Characteristics of Achievers..................................10
Underachiever Profiles 11
The Rebel 12
The Conformist..13
The Stressed Learner 14
The Struggling Student..15
The Victim..16
The Distracted Learner..17
The Bored Student 18
The Complacent Learner 19
The Single-Sided Achiever 20

THE COACHES 21

Six Ways to Promote and Support Student Motivation 22
Teachers as Academic Coaches..23
Classrooms that Support Achievement 23
Thirteen Positive Coaching Tips for Teachers 25
Eight Teaching Pitfalls and How to Avoid Them 29
Parents as Academic Coaches...32
Homes that Support Achievement..32
Eleven Positive Coaching Tips for Parents 34
Eight Parenting Pitfalls and How to Avoid Them 37

THE STRATEGY SESSIONS 41

The School Review 42
The Student Self-Assessment 42
The Student Interview 45
Tips for Successful Student Interviews 45
Questions for Student Interviews..47
The Parent Interview 49
Questions for Parent Interviews...49
The Teacher Conference 50
Questions for Teacher Conferences...50
The Action Plan 52
Action Plan Part A: The Academic Profile 52
Action Plan Part B: The Problem Checklist...55

SUCCESS BOOSTERS 61

What Are Success Boosters?..62
The First Step: Breaking the Failure Cycle 62
Learning 63
Identifying Appropriate Learning
(Is School Too Easy for the Student, or Too Hard?)...............................63
Developing a Value for Learning
(Is Learning Important to the Student?) 66
Identifying Learning Style
(How Does the Student Learn Best?)..68
Developing Study Habits 70
The Space 71
The Schedule..71
What to Study...72
The Essentials 75
The Methods 76
Managing School Work 78
Setting Goals...79
Eleven Steps to Successful Goal Setting...80

Dealing with Personal Issues 85
Self-Esteem 85
Perfectionism 89
Friends 93
Stress 97
Power and Control 99
Health Issues 100

THE CONTRACT 103

Action Plan Part C: The Commitment to Action 104
Completing the Contract 105
How to Handle Reluctant Players 111
How to Talk with Resistant Students 111
A Few Final Encouraging Words 112

RESOURCES 113

Rating Your Classroom 115
Rating Your Home Environment 116
Help for School Problems 117
Teacher Work Management Form: Weekly Syllabus (Sample) 119
Teacher Work Management Form: Monthly Calendar (Sample) 120
Student Work Plan 1 (Sample) 121
Student Work Plan 1 (Blank) 122
Student Work Plan 2 (Blank) 123
Student Work Plan 3 (Blank) 124
Student Work Plan 4 (Blank) 126

References 127
Index 129
About the Author 134

INTRODUCTION

Which group of characteristics describes a learner you know?

1	2
enthusiastic and willing to try	*frustrated*
concerned and conscientious	*unsure*
motivated	*complacent*
attentive	*irresponsible*
well-organized	*poor risk taker*
a self-starter	*procrastinates*
task-oriented	*daydreams*
goes the extra mile	*defensive*
confident	*distracted*
competitive	*bored*

If you are a teacher or parent of the first kind of learner, you can rejoice in how well the student is playing—and winning—the school achievement game. He or she is experiencing the positive rewards of school success, building feelings of personal and academic confidence and competence.

If you're reading this book, however, chances are that you are a teacher or parent of the second kind of learner. You have either led or attended conferences where someone has said, "So-and-so has a lot of ability; it's just not being shown in school." Either the student doesn't know how to play the school achievement game or is choosing not to play it. He or she is trapped in the underachievement cycle. Failure leads to negative feelings about self and school, which lead to continued failure.

A Widespread Problem

Articles in our newspapers, magazines, and educational journals remind us of our national concern for students who are falling behind in school and in learning. Academic underachievement is so widespread that communities and states across the country are demanding school reform and restructure. And while many people may think of low-ability or "troubled" students as the ones who are most at risk, this is not always the case. Anywhere from 5 to 50 percent of students identified as gifted and talented are also called underachievers.

Not all children can or should be straight-A students, since everyone differs in their abilities and interests. But *all children have the potential to learn and to personally succeed in school.*

Over the past several years, I have worked closely with parents and teachers of students who have the ability to do well in school but are failing miserably. I have also worked closely with the students. And I have come to realize that *underachievers want school to be different.* Some are angry, some are hurt, nearly all have negative feelings about themselves, but they still have a desire to be successful in school. They simply don't know how.

Jim's Story

Jim's story is a good example of how some students get trapped in the under-achievement cycle—and how, with appropriate intervention and help, they can break that cycle and become personally successful.

When Jim entered kindergarten, he was already reading at the sixth-grade level. His kindergarten teacher didn't know what to do with such an advanced reader, so she had him practice words printed on index cards. I believe that this is when Jim first decided that school was not for him.

By the time Jim was in fourth grade, he was the kid with the reputation. Any playground disturbance or rule infraction in the cafeteria led to Jim being called to the principal's office. Every day in his math class, he refused to finish his assignments. He would complete just enough problems, in his opinion, to show his teacher that he "got it," then skip the rest.

As a consequence, Jim was not allowed to go out for recess and was given detention time in the classroom to finish his work. His name was a permanent entry on the detention roster. His grades reflected his lack of effort and late work.

In high school, Jim thought that he had finally figured out the system. He wanted to be free from class lectures that he found boring and repetitive; he wanted to be able to work independently on his class assignments. So he discovered in-school suspension. Whenever he broke a school rule, he was punished by being sent to a work space outside of the classroom. To Jim, this was no punishment. It was exactly what he wanted!

When I began working with Jim, my first task was to try to convince him that in-school suspension was not a good thing. Next, Jim, his parents, his teachers, and I worked together to identify what appeared to be the causes of Jim's lack of academic success. (I say "causes" instead of "cause" because in the majority of interventions I have done with underachievers, there has been more than one reason for a student's school problems.) Then, still in partnership, we developed a plan of action that would lead toward positive change.

Our plan of action called for Jim to focus on one area at a time. He did, and he began to build some successes. His attitudes about school slowly improved. Even more importantly, his feelings about himself, his abilities, and his potential went from negative to positive. As the obstacles for his school success were removed, Jim's climb up from underachievement continued.

Who Is Responsible?

Who is responsible for students' academic success or failure—parents, teachers, or students themselves? Some people say that student achievement relies most on a supportive home environment and parental priorities. Others claim that the teacher who controls the learning determines the outcomes. Still others insist that the motivation to learn and succeed must come from within the child.

From my experience in working with underachievers, I believe that student success and failure depend on all three: parents, teachers, and students. True, teachers and parents provide the learning environment, the support systems, and the modeling for achievement that students need to succeed. However, the student's own learning abilities, interests, academic skills, work and study habits, and personal issues such as self-esteem, stress, and perfectionism also have a direct bearing on his or her school performance.

It is not always possible for parents, teachers, and students to work together on a plan for change. But it is almost always preferable.

Partnerships for Positive Change

I have learned through working with underachieving kids that positive change is more likely to occur if partnerships are formed that involve the school *and* the home. It's best when parents, teachers, and students cooperate to identify the causes for lack of school success and develop a plan for change.

That is why this book was written for parents, teachers, and students, not just one or the other. It is my hope that all three will read it and use it together. Because this is not always possible, I have identified each section so a parent, teacher, or student can easily find and use the ideas and strategies appropriate for him or her.

In the pages that follow, you'll come to know some of the causes for student underachievement. You'll learn about homes and classrooms that support and encourage student success. If your child is currently doing well in school, you'll discover more ways to keep a good thing going. If you are a parent or teacher of an underachiever, you'll find out how to form partnerships and work together to design plans for positive change.

The underachievement intervention process described here has been proven effective with students of all ages, from first grade through high school. I know it can work for your student, too.

How Long Will It Take for Change?

How long will it take before you can start seeing changes in your student's school success? That depends on three factors.

▶ First, it depends on the number of underachievement causes. I once had a student whose only cause for lack of school success was school-related stress. After working through some strategies for dealing with stress, she pulled out of her academic slump within the month.

When several causes exist, each needs to be worked on and conquered separately. This may take several weeks, or the entire school year. You will need to work together on one problem at a time.

▶ Second, it depends on how long the student has been underachieving. Students don't develop underachieving habits overnight, or even over a summer vacation. It stands to reason that the sooner you catch these habits developing, the faster they can be reversed.

For students who have been underachieving for a considerable length of time (more than one school year), it will take longer to break the cycle of failure and build success in school.

▶ Finally, it depends on the quality of the partnerships formed between parents, teachers, and the student. Everyone needs to agree on a plan for change. Everyone needs to consistently hold to the plan, giving it time to work. This calls for persistence, commitment, and a genuine belief that school can and will be better.

For some of you, this book will bring a "quick fix" for your student's school achievement problems. For others with more complex issues, that process will take longer—maybe a quarter of the school year, maybe even the entire school year. Don't get discouraged! Remember that all journeys begin with a single step. But if you don't bravely take that step, there may be no progress at all.

It won't always be easy. Depending on the individual student's history and experience, there may be times when nothing you do will seem to make any difference. Keep trying. Helping a young learner to recognize, develop, and use his or her talents and abilities is a lifelong gift. Remember that your learner wants school to be different. Working together, you can make it so.

Diane Heacox
Minneapolis, Minnesota

HOW TO USE THIS BOOK

Up from Underachievement describes a step-by-step program for intervening with underachievement and promoting student success. Teachers and parents learn specific ways to support achievement and create a positive learning environment. Students learn specific ways to set goals, manage their work, develop good study habits, and boost their own self-esteem. Together, they develop a plan for action that clearly outlines everyone's responsibilities.

Because of the way the program is presented, it's best if teachers and parents read the entire book. You may find helpful suggestions in sections that don't at first appear to apply to your particular student. After an initial reading, you can return to the sections listed below for ideas tailored to your student's circumstances and needs.

For students using this book, it's best to have help from a parent, a teacher, or both. But even if you don't have adult support, you can still follow the program and benefit from it. Just refer to the sections marked "Students" below and on page 8. Follow these instructions to guide your use of the book.

If a Student Is Currently Succeeding in School...

▲ Teachers and Parents

1. Review The Coaches (pages 21–40).
2. Read Success Boosters (pages 61–101) for suggestions that seem appropriate for your student. If you are a teacher, review the sections marked "Teachers." If you are a parent, be sure to see the ideas in the sections marked "Parents."

▲ Students

Read Success Boosters (pages 61–101) to learn ways you can do even better in school. Pay special attention to the sections marked "Students."

If a Student Is Underachieving in School...

1. Review The Players (pages 9–20).

2. Review The Coaches (pages 21–40).

3. Conduct a Student Interview (pages 45–48) and/or have the student do the Self-Assessment (pages 42–44). Check your student's responses in Help for School Problems (pages 117–118).

4. Conduct a Parent Interview (pages 49–50) by meeting with the parent or talking by telephone.

5. Complete the Academic Profile (Part A of the Action Plan, pages 52–54).

6. Review the Players' Prescriptives (page 56).

7. Complete the Problem Checklist (Part B of the Action Plan, pages 57–59).

8. Using the information from the completed Problem Checklist, refer to sections in Success Boosters (pages 61–101) that apply to your student. Be sure to see those marked "Teachers."

9. Using the ideas from Success Boosters, work with the student (and, if possible, the parent) to complete the Commitment to Action (Part C of the Action Plan, pages 104–110). You will then have a contract listing specific goals for positive change.

10. Follow the plan, be consistent, and stick with it!

1. Review The Players (pages 9–20).

2. Review The Coaches (pages 21–40).

3. Conduct a Student Interview (pages 45–48) and/or have the student do a Self-Assessment (pages 42–44). Check your student's responses in Help for School Problems (pages 117–118).

4. Request and attend a Teacher Conference (pages 50–51).

5. Complete the Academic Profile (Part A of the Action Plan, pages 52–54).

6. Review the Players' Prescriptives (page 56).

7. Complete the Problem Checklist (Part B of the Action Plan, pages 57–59).

8. Using the information from the completed Problem Checklist, refer to sections in Success Boosters (pages 61–101) that apply to your student. Be sure to see those marked "Parents."

9. Using the ideas from Success Boosters, work with the student (and, if possible, the teacher) to complete the Commitment to Action (Part C of the Action Plan, pages 104–110). You will then have a contract listing specific goals for positive change.

10. Follow the plan, be consistent, and stick with it!

▲ Students

1. Read The Players (pages 9–20).

2. Do the Student Self-Assessment (pages 42–44). Check your responses in Help for School Problems (pages 117–118).

3. Read the Success Boosters (pages 61–101) that match the problems you discovered through the self-assessment. Pay special attention to those marked "Students."

4. Read Setting Goals (pages 79–82).

5. Using the goal-setting plan on pages 83–84, write one goal for yourself that will help you with one of your school problems. Work on that goal.

6. When you have accomplished your first goal, write and work on another. Keep going until you have made positive changes in all of the areas you want to improve.

THE
PLAYERS

Eight Characteristics of Achievers

Think of the people you know. Picture one you would definitely describe as an achiever—a success.

This person may be an adult you know socially, someone you work with, or a professional you come into contact with for one reason or another. He or she may be your auto mechanic, your physician, your high school coach, a neighbor, a parent, a musician—anyone you choose. Or this person may be a student who is achieving in school.

When you picture this individual, what personal characteristics do you notice? See if you agree with these.

1. *Achievers are goal-oriented.* They set long- or short-term goals and move toward them. Their goals are both personal and professional (or academic).

2. *Achievers are positive thinkers.* They expect that they will be successful. They have already experienced enough success in their lives that they are sure they can continue to do well.

3. *Achievers are confident.* They have strong, positive feelings about their abilities. For this reason, they are able to risk trying out new ideas or methods.

4. *Achievers are resilient.* They do not let failure (small "f" or big "F") get them down. They bounce back from defeat and try again. They value improvement but are not disabled if their performance is less than perfect.

5. *Achievers have self-discipline.* They have the ability and drive to stay on task in both their personal and professional/academic goals. They resist distractions and diversions.

6. *Achievers have pride.* They are proud of their accomplishments. They know they have done well, and they believe they have the right to feel good about themselves. These individuals develop a sense of inner satisfaction. They are less dependent on others to say "well done."

7. *Achievers are proficient.* They have the necessary skills to be successful. Whether they are students with basic learning skills, engineers with mechanical skills, or doctors with diagnostic skills, they have what they need to do well.

8. *Achievers are risk takers.* They are willing to work on the edge. They are able to try new things and push the limits of what is known. Risk taking requires courage and confidence in one's abilities; achievers have both.

Surprisingly, the underachieving student may have some of these characteristics; they are just not evident in school. Many individuals who are not academically successful have outside interests where their talents and abilities shine. There are plenty of so-called "poor students" who blossom when the final bell rings. They are computer whiz kids, accomplished musicians and dancers, active volunteers in their church or community organizations. Just because they don't perform well in school doesn't mean they can't perform at all—a fact that's important to remember and keep remembering.

Underachiever Profiles

In observing and working with students who underachieve, I have developed several broad characterizations of those who can't or won't play the school game. I include them here, not because they should be used to label students, but because they can enhance our understanding of certain behaviors and characteristics. Teachers and parents may recognize students they are concerned about; students will realize that their problems are not unique, and they are not alone.

The Rebel

"This is dumb."

"Why do we have to do this anyway?"

"This doesn't make any sense."

"This is a total waste of time."

"I have more important things to do."

"I will not do that just because you want me to."

"I don't care if you won't let me do it."

"I don't care if you won't let me have it."

"WHY SHOULD I PLAY THE SCHOOL GAME?"

The Rebel doesn't see the relevance of classroom activities and assignments. She refuses to believe that there is any connection between school and the "real world." She has a general "I-don't-need-this" attitude.

This student may have unrealistic visions of the future, especially when it comes to career aspirations. She may dream of a glamour job—rock musician, professional athlete, artist, actor. She may see school learning as unnecessary for success in her chosen field.

There may also be a power struggle going on between this student and the adults in her life. Parents may insist that she do well in school so she can get into college and aim for a career more to their liking than hers. Teachers may push advanced course work or academic goals without finding out what she wants—and is willing—to do. In either case, The Rebel keeps control of the situation by refusing to comply with adult wishes. Parents and teachers may retaliate by taking away privileges, limiting her freedom, or punishing her in some other way. She retains power by simply not producing in school.

▲ ▲ ▲ ▲

It's easy to recognize Shayna in the hallways of her senior high school. She's the student dressed all in black, loaded down with junk jewelry, toting a bulging tapestry bag. She routinely either walks out of classes she finds "uninteresting" and "not worth her time," or she is asked to leave due to her confrontive behavior and refusal to do the work.

Shayna wants to be either an author or an actress. She claims that her high school courses are "not necessary" for her chosen career. However, when you ask Shayna what she is doing to prepare for her future, she tells you that she has not registered for her high school's creative writing course ("there are too many deadlines; I can't write that way"). She has also never participated in any of her school's drama productions and, in fact, has not acted in a play since the summer after fourth grade.

▲ ▲ ▲ ▲

The Conformist

"I don't want to be a nerd."

"All of my friends did the same on the test."

"If I get done early, it just means more work."

"The best part of school is seeing my friends."

"If I want a date to homecoming...."

"I just don't want to work that hard."

"The regular math class is better than the honors class."

"But I won't have time for baseball practice."

"If I do too well, I'll get teased."

"DON'T NOTICE THAT I AM SMART."

The Conformist has decided that doing well in school is just not worth it. He may have found out in the elementary grades that those who finished first and did the best got more work as a reward for their efforts. Maybe he discovered that working slowly filled up the time, or that doing fine (but not great) work was a way to avoid the dreaded and deadly "enrichment" projects dreamed up by his teachers. In any event, he learned early and well that more is not better where school work is concerned.

Some students choose to do less than their best because of peer pressure; they want to blend in with their friends, not stand out from them. The Conformist tries to hide his abilities because he fears being labeled a "nerd." If he is athletic, he would rather be known as a "jock" than a "brain." (Conformist girls may believe that they must choose between being smart and being popular, especially with boys.)

This student is more comfortable when adults don't expect too much from him. ("If I get an A on this paper, my parents or teachers may expect me to do it all the time!") He conceals his abilities and opts for mediocrity. He lives a lie to protect himself from peer ostracism and adult demands.

▲ ▲ ▲ ▲

Damen is in the sixth grade. One October day, he tells me that since the beginning of the school year, he has cut down his responses in class discussions from an average of seven to an average of five.

"What's going on?" I ask.

"The other kids let me know when to stop," he says.

"How do they do it?"

"Well," he explains, "besides the teasing during and after class, they sigh and move around in their chairs. Then I know it's time to be quiet."

▲ ▲ ▲ ▲

The Stressed Learner

"It's not quite ready yet."

"I could have done better if I had more time."

"I was sure I could do well with that assignment."

"If I keep it one more day, it will be so much better that I can make up the points I lose for being late."

"What if I can't do it?"

"She's not a very good teacher. She gave me a decent grade on that paper I put together at the last minute."

"I'll work on it later."

"IT'S NOT GOOD ENOUGH."

The Stressed Learner is often known by another name: The Perfectionist. Her self-esteem rises and falls depending on her most recent academic performance. When she is first and best, she feels great. When she is not on top, she berates herself with "should haves."

Over time, perfectionism can lead to paralysis of performance. The Stressed Learner stops trying to achieve out of fear of making a mistake. She procrastinates because she believes that she can't perform well enough. She is a poor risk taker, always choosing the class activity or assignment that seems to offer the greatest chance for success rather than challenge. She distrusts positive comments from others because their standards are "not as high" as hers. If something looks hard, she quits before giving it a fair chance.

She is less productive than she might be because she spends too much time revising her work. She may even decide not to turn in a completed report or assignment because "it's not good enough."

The Perfectionist doesn't reward improvement. All that matters is being Number 1. Personally, she experiences more punishments than rewards. As a result, her academic performance may stall over time.

▲▲▲▲

Jenny's third-grade teacher makes a practice of helping Jenny sort through her book bag, locker, and desk. Together, they often retrieve papers that are done to the teacher's standards, but Jenny doesn't want to turn them in because "they aren't perfect yet."

▲▲▲▲

The Struggling Student

"I don't understand."

"It's too hard for me."

"I don't understand what the teacher wants me to do."

"I forgot."

"I used to be smart."

"That's too much work to do; I'll never get it done in time."

"I thought that was what we were supposed to do."

"I JUST DON'T GET IT."

The Struggling Student may have been the bright child who was able to slide through the elementary grades without learning much new. At some point, however, he hit the wall when the content became new and demanding enough to require study skills. Since he never had to learn how to study, he may perceive his lack of success as a loss of intelligence. In fact, he doesn't know the basics of how to learn, how to manage his time and assignments, and how to organize his work load.

Some Struggling Students fall within the gray areas of learning disabilities. Educators and parents recognize that something is keeping these children from learning, but the children are not "disabled enough" to receive special assistance in school. While these students may not be "disabled" *per se*, they may have learning deficits—or learning differences—which affect their school performance. Because direct intervention and assistance in remediating or coping with the deficits are not provided, the children continue to struggle in school. Their self-esteem plunges, and everyone's expectations for their performance—their teachers', their parents', and their own—are artificially lowered. Over time, Struggling Students begin to look below average in their potential to learn.

▲▲▲▲

Michael's parents and teacher are meeting with the school psychologist because the teacher believes that Michael has a learning disability. Michael is now in third grade and is still struggling to read. Sounding out unfamiliar words is impossible for him.

"Michael seldom pays attention in class," the teacher complains, "and it's a struggle to get him to even pick up a pencil." The teacher goes on to note that Michael is in the bottom third of his class.

"We tested Michael," the psychologist reports. "The results indicate that he has abstract thinking abilities in the superior range, and verbal abilities in the high average range."

"Performance is what I see," the teacher argues, "and I see a low average child."

▲▲▲▲

The Victim

"If you'd given me more time, I would have gotten it done."

"The assignment was just too hard for me."

"Our family wasn't home last night, so I couldn't do my homework."

"I have gymnastics practice on Tuesdays."

"If you would quit pushing me, I might get it done."

"You expected too much."

"I couldn't find the book you asked me to read."

"No one ever taught me to do that."

"The teacher doesn't like me."

"IT'S NOT MY FAULT."

The Victim is reluctant to accept responsibility for her lack of school success. She has used every excuse in the book for why her work isn't done or is done in an inferior manner. She may have been a child given too much power at too early an age. She is definitely in control now.

This student may have had adults managing her school work rather than personally taking responsibility for it. For example, her teacher may have called her parents weekly to discuss the student's performance. There may have been notes going back and forth between school and home for months; there may have been several parent-teacher conferences related to the child's lack of effort. Meanwhile, the student has been able to sit back and watch everyone else work through a plan of action and own the problem. A learner so successful in manipulating significant adults probably can also manage her own work.

▲▲▲▲

Julie's mother and fifth-grade teacher have an elaborate system of note-writing for reporting her late or missing work. If Julie doesn't do her work, the teacher sends a note home to Mom, describing the incomplete assignments and attaching any necessary handouts or worksheets. She also checks to make sure that Julie has the appropriate books when she leaves the classroom.

Sometimes Julie rushes off for the bus before checking out with her teacher. Other times, she conveniently "forgets" her note at school. No homework means more time for television.

▲▲▲▲

The Distracted Learner

"I worked last night until 10:00."

"We had a track meet."

"Something came up at home."

"Things haven't been going real well lately."

"Do you think I could get an extension on the due date?"

"This was my weekend to spend with my dad."

"I JUST CAN'T HANDLE IT ALL."

The Distracted Learner is the individual with personal problems or concerns that affect his school performance. Factors that influence his ability to focus may include adjusting to a new school, a new brother or sister, his parents' separation or divorce, a new marriage or living situation, or chemical dependency within the family.

This student may be experiencing stress or anxiety for very personal reasons of which the school may be unaware. Or he may be distracted because of competition for his time. If the student has a job, is involved in several extracurricular activities, and/or is responsible for supervising younger family members and doing other tasks at home, there may simply not be enough hours in the day for school work, too.

In adolescence, friendships and other personal relationships often take precedence over school matters. The Distracted Learner may be in the process of formulating personal decisions, judgments, and values that seem far more important than today's math assignment. Problems with chemical dependency, depression, eating disorders, and conflicting sexual values may make school work appear irrelevant.

▲▲▲▲

Chris's mother works the evening shift, so he takes care of his younger sister and brothers every school night. By the time he helps them with their homework, fixes and feeds them dinner, cleans up the kitchen, and gets everyone ready for bed, it's 9:00 or later. Only then does he have quiet time for his own homework—and he's often too tired to do it.

▲▲▲▲

The Bored Student

"I learned all this last year."

"How many times do we have to go over this?"

"Why can't the other kids understand this, so we can go on to something else?"

"When do we get to do the hard stuff?"

"I get so tired of the same thing every day."

"When can I learn what I want to learn?"

"I'd like to do it another way."

"THERE'S NOTHING NEW AND EXCITING TO LEARN."

The Bored Student may be one who truly needs more challenging activities due to her advanced skills and abilities. Students who enter school with advanced skills may wait for years until the curriculum catches up with their learning needs. By then, they have formed sloppy work habits and lazy learning patterns.

Other students may say they are bored when they are really afraid of failure. They may decide that the work is too difficult and choose to stay uninvolved. Failing because you don't do the work is better than failing when you do.

Still other students who are struggling to learn may simply give up and use boredom as a rationale for their lack of success.

The Bored Student must be looked at carefully to determine the underlying causes of her refrain. Is she using it as an excuse for her lack of effort in the learning process? Is it a defense for the poor quality of her work? Is the work really too easy?

▲ ▲ ▲ ▲

For the past year, Maria has had reading problems. Her teacher reports that she is falling behind in class. Maria's mother and father encourage her to read for fun (and, they hope, to develop her skills). But whenever they suggest a trip to the library, they meet with resistance. Maria doesn't want to go to the library. Reading, she insists, is "boring."

▲ ▲ ▲ ▲

The Complacent Learner

"I'm doing as well as I want to do."

"I'm satisfied. I don't know why you aren't."

"Quit pressuring me."

"You're never satisfied with how I do."

"This class is just right for me. I don't want to be in the enriched class."

"It's important to you, not me."

"Sure, I could have done better."

"I'M DOING JUST FINE."

The Complacent Learner seems basically content with how school and his learning are going. He likes himself and doesn't seem to have any academic problems that slow him down. However, the adults in his life believe that he could do better in school, if only he tried.

For now, the student is satisfied. It is the teacher or parent whose attitudes, standards, and expectations are not being met. Sometimes the adult's goals are unrealistic for the child. Other times, they reflect a value system the child does not share.

The Complacent Learner may dig in his heels or fight back when these ideas are forced on him, or he may learn just to put up with the nagging. Either way, he will continue on in his own achievement pattern. In time, he may decide that it's worth it to buckle down if something interesting comes along, or if there's something he wants to do that hinges on his school performance.

▲ ▲ ▲ ▲

Manuel doesn't understand why his parents and teachers won't leave him alone. He gets mostly C's, and he's perfectly satisfied—after all, that's average, isn't it? But the adults keep insisting that he could do better. His achievement test scores are always high, they remind him, and he could probably get straight A's if he tried. The trouble is, he doesn't want to.

However, he does want to go to camp this summer, and his parents have made it clear that this year, camp will depend on improvement in his grades. When his final report card comes in, they're pleased to see that Manuel has gotten all A's and B's.

▲ ▲ ▲ ▲

The Single-Sided Achiever

"That class isn't important to me."

"That subject bores me."

"I only like certain classes."

"This class is different."

"I just can't get motivated about that subject."

"This class doesn't teach me anything I want to know."

"IT DOESN'T INTEREST ME."

The Single-Sided Achiever has decided that only certain classes are worthy of her attention and energy. She may be intensely interested in one or two subjects, and these are the ones where she's willing to work. She chooses to achieve in some classes and to underachieve in others.

She may be motivated by the subject matter, teaching style, or learning activities of the classes she achieves in. Others are dismissed as "boring" or "useless."

The Single-Sided Achiever is rigid in her opinions and actions. She may focus on one area and fail to develop or even discover other talents she may have.

▲ ▲ ▲ ▲

Yolanda has seen herself as a scientist since age three, when she first became fascinated with dinosaurs. Her science passion consumes all of her free time, as well as any unplanned moments in school. Her teachers often find her absorbed in her projects, collections, and readings during her other academic subjects. Despite their efforts, they are unable to channel Yolanda's energy or attention toward learning anything else.

▲ ▲ ▲ ▲

THE
COACHES

Six Ways to Promote and Support Student Motivation

As you were reading through the Underachiever Profiles, you may have been sensitive to the stories-behind-the-stories: the students' interactions with the adults in their lives. It's true that teachers and parents can strongly influence a student's motivation or lack of motivation. But does that mean that one or the other should be blamed for a student's failure to achieve? In most cases, no. Parents, teachers—and students themselves—seem to be equally involved. That's why *Up from Underachievement* stresses a partnership among all three.

Motivation is an individual's need or desire to achieve a particular goal. It is necessary for success in the classroom, on the soccer field, in business, in personal relationships—in virtually every human endeavor. You cannot give a child motivation; it must come from within. But you can certainly promote it and support it.

1. ***Be a model of achievement yourself.*** Show what it's like to set goals, reach them, and feel good about it.

2. ***Introduce the student to other adults who are achievers in his areas of interest.*** Your young writer may enjoy meeting a local author. Your future pilot might relish a visit with a neighbor who served in the Air Force or works for a commercial airline.

3. ***Communicate your expectations to the student.*** Clearly state what you want her to do. For example, it is not enough to say, "You have to study every night." Instead, you need to say, "I expect you to use 30 uninterrupted minutes for learning every night."

4. ***Give the student some "how-to" help on getting motivated.*** Encourage him to choose school projects that match his interests. For example, Jason loves to act. When he was given a school assignment to do a biographical report, his guardian suggested that he do a video interview with a historical character—Jason himself, dressed up and playing the role. Jason cleared the idea with his teacher and turned in an excellent project.

5. ***Make sure the student has time to develop and practice the skills necessary for success.*** Even a highly motivated child will have trouble learning if her days are consumed by music lessons, sports, chores, and other activities. Leave time each day for homework—preferably a regular time in a regular place.

6. ***Encourage and praise learning efforts.*** Recognize improvements, large and small. Hurrahs, hugs, and pats on the back can contribute significantly to a student's motivation to learn.

Motivation, success, and achievement are closely linked to one another. Students are more likely to be successful if they put forth their best effort. Once successful, they are motivated toward their next goal. In the end, they come to believe they are capable. They expect positive results for their own efforts. They have become achievers.

Parents and teachers cannot make a child motivated to learn. However, they can be skilled and active *academic coaches*, creating home and school environments that enhance the child's chances of being motivated.

Teachers as Academic Coaches

Classrooms that Support Achievement

In researching academic motivation, Joanne Rand Whitmore identified two factors that critically influence a child's ability to be successful in school: the child's self-esteem, and how well the learning in school matches what the child is capable of learning.

As an academic coach, you can address both factors within the classroom setting. The environment of your classroom can support the development of self-esteem, or it can slowly erode it. Whether the curriculum meets student needs is under your direct control. Generally speaking, classroom learning activities should not be so low-level that they provide insufficient challenge. Naturally, they also should not be so difficult that students never experience success.

How would you rate your own academic coaching abilities? How well is achievement supported in your classroom? Find out by completing the survey that follows. Mark items "true" if they describe your classroom, "false" if they do not. Keep in mind that some of the characteristics listed are positive, and some are negative.

After completing the survey, check your responses in Rating Your Classroom on page 115.

✎ TEACHER SURVEY

	TRUE	FALSE
1. Most of my lessons involve my presentation of information or skills.	☐	☐
2. I give my students opportunities to share what they know about a topic.	☐	☐
3. I design a single set of learning goals for all of my students.	☐	☐
4. Students feel secure and free from threat in my classroom.	☐	☐
5. I pretest my students so I understand what each of them knows and needs to learn. I adjust my lessons accordingly.	☐	☐
6. I have a specific and unchanging daily or weekly routine in my classroom.	☐	☐
7. I have a system to help my students keep track of their assignments and deadlines.	☐	☐
8. Students who do not complete their work are not allowed to participate in certain activities or opportunities. (In the elementary grades, this may involve keeping children in for recess; in the secondary grades, it may involve keeping students out of accelerated or enriched classes.)	☐	☐
9. I recognize the successes of individual students.	☐	☐
10. The majority of my remarks on my student's papers are positive.	☐	☐
11. I have individual or private conferences with students who are having problems in class.	☐	☐
12. I use contracts with students who are having school problems.	☐	☐
13. I give my students examples of how their learning is used in the "real world."	☐	☐
14. I tell my students why a topic or skill is important to learn.	☐	☐
15. I get students interested in a topic by posing questions or providing unique information that will get them curious.	☐	☐
16. My teaching techniques tend to stay the same.	☐	☐
17. The objectives I develop are for my own planning and use; I don't share them with my students.	☐	☐
18. I grade most learning activities so my students understand that their assignments are important.	☐	☐
19. I recognize students when they improve in a subject or learning activity. I compliment them on their achievements, special talents, and abilities.	☐	☐
20. I regularly plan activities designed to develop my students' positive self-esteem.	☐	☐

Thirteen Positive Coaching Tips for Teachers

1. FOCUS ON THE POSITIVE

As the old song goes, "accentuate the positive." Keep your comments on your students' papers as positive as possible. Recognize good thinking or a creative approach. If nothing else, comment on their elegant handwriting.

Think of ways to recognize individuals in your classroom, perhaps through student-of-the-week activities, positive letters home, or class recognition of students who have improved in particular subjects or activities. Put your positive plans into action.

Use positive incentives for good work skills rather than punishments for not meeting requirements. (Keeping children in for recess works in some cases, but in others it leads to power struggles.) When you offer an incentive, present it in a positive way. For example, say, "If you get your math work done today...," not "If you *don't* get your math work done today...."

Denying a qualified child an opportunity to move to a higher reading group or a more advanced class because of poor work skills is unfair. It is also counterproductive. Many teachers report that poor work habits disappear when students are given a greater challenge.

2. KEEP PROBLEMS PRIVATE

Hold private conferences with students who are experiencing difficulties in school. Set up contracts with those who need direct intervention. Replace public classroom encounters with personal, one-on-one conversations.

If a student is having problems, ask him to meet with you before or after class. Use "I"-statements to get your message and feelings across. For example, you might say something like, "I am disappointed that you did not have your assignments ready for the last two days. Is there something going on right now that is keeping you from your work? What can you do to solve this problem so your next assignment will be on time?"

3. GET THEM INVOLVED

Students' motivation and interest will be higher if you involve them in the learning process. Provide opportunities for individual students to share what they know about your topic. For example, you might let them brainstorm what they know about the topic of the next social studies unit before you begin. Have them list questions they would like to have answered. What do they want to know more about? Tailor your units to the needs, interests, and knowledge of your students.

Give them opportunities to share their passions, even those which may not fit into your curriculum. For example, you might ask your current events scholar to do a weekly news update. Or set aside some time each week to spotlight one student. Encourage the student to share a current interest with the class in an informal format.

When you recognize your students' knowledge and encourage them to get actively involved in their own learning, you also build their self-esteem.

4. PROVIDE VARIETY

Predictable daily or weekly routines are boring for students *and* teachers. If your fourth graders know that every Monday they will do the vocabulary for their reading story, every Tuesday they will read the story, every Wednesday they will answer questions on the story, and every Thursday and Friday they will do skill sheets, where's the anticipation? If your social studies class knows that each day you will lecture for 30 minutes and they will read or do seat work for 25 minutes, where's the excitement?

There is another good reason to provide variety: Not all of your students learn in the same way. Some need hands-on activities; others learn best by seeing or hearing. Some students prefer a step-by-step approach; others are more self-directed and favor activities that give them choices. Vary your lessons so that each of your students has some opportunities to learn in the way he or she prefers.

Allow your students to select learning activities from a list of possibilities reflecting a broad range of learning styles and ways to share and learn information. Encourage them to come up with their own activities. For example, you might have them brainstorm a list of 20 end-of-the-unit projects, with the last item being "come up with your own." (Find out more about learning styles on pages 68–70.)

5. GIVE THEM TOOLS FOR SUCCESS

Some students are clueless when it comes to organizing their work and keeping track of assignments and due dates. Help them by providing a class method for tracking their work. (Find specific suggestions on pages 78–79.)

It's possible that some of your students have never developed study skills. Give them opportunities to learn how to learn. Teach study skills to *all* of your students, regardless of their ability and current success in school. (Find ideas on pages 70–78.)

Allow time for your students to tell or show one another how they thought through a problem, came up with an answer, or arrived at a solution. Call "share time" after activities that use creative thinking. Your students will begin to recognize the broad range of ideas in their classroom.

Introduce them to thinking and problem-solving strategies that develop their independence. Teach them specific strategies and processes; use real problems for practice. For example, you might have your students generate a list of current problems in their school, neighborhood, or community, then choose one to work on.

6. MAKE LEARNING REAL

Give real-life examples showing how school learning relates to the real world. This may help remedy the lack of motivation some students feel—the "we-don't-really-need-this-because-we'll-never-use-it" attitude. For example, you might apply mathematics skills to balancing a checkbook, or show how geometry is applied to architecture. Bring in guest speakers to point out the connections between school learning and job skills.

Your students will be more motivated by activities that teach content or skills they perceive as worth learning. It is important for you as an academic coach to examine your course content from this perspective. Keep the meaningful; drop the meaningless from your lesson plans.

7. ADJUST YOUR CURRICULUM

Be aware of what individual students already know and what they need to know in your classroom. Pretest your students on the knowledge and skills of the upcoming unit. Eliminate repetitive drill-and-practice exercises for students who show mastery of the material. Replace these exercises with appropriately challenging activities for your most able students. For students who need additional time and assistance to learn the material, provide suitable remediation activities.

Your lessons should directly reflect what the individual student *needs* to learn. Lockstep, everyone-turn-to-the-same-page instruction addresses the needs of only those few children who are at that level of learning.

8. GET THEM INTERESTED

Show the importance and relevance of new learning by telling your students how it applies to earlier information, or how it can be used. If a topic is already somewhat familiar, introduce the lesser known or more unusual aspects to avoid the "we-already-know-this" complaint. So they learned about the Civil War last year; what new perspectives are they ready for, now that they are older? If there is something especially amazing or intriguing about the topic, use it to hook students into learning more.

Pose questions at the beginning of a lesson so students can look or listen for the answers or clues to the answers. For example, you might ask them to think about Lincoln's decisions concerning the South as they read their history text. Then ask, "Would you have handled the situation in the same way? Why or why not?"

9. MAKE LEARNING APPROPRIATE

Make abstract information more concrete by showing objects or pictures, doing demonstrations, giving examples, or having students explore the topic, conduct the experiment, or put the idea into their own words. Provide detailed descriptions so your students can form mental pictures of a concept or idea.

For example, you might take your class on a visual journey through the circulatory system by saying something like, "Imagine that you are a blood cell. You are inside your own body, racing through an artery at top speed....Now I will tell you what you see as you travel through your circulatory system...."

10. LET THEM IN ON YOUR OBJECTIVES

Tell your students your reasons for believing that a topic or skill is important to learn. Explain what they are going to learn and why they are going to learn it. You may wish to give them a syllabus or outline of your topic, so they can see how all the lessons fit together.

11. MINIMIZE EVALUATION

Plan many of your activities to focus on learning rather than evaluation. You want your students to experience the joy of learning for its own sake. They should not have to view every activity as a way to fill in a blank in a grade book.

Try letting your students self-evaluate their projects. Ask questions like, "What surprised you? What interested you? What do you want to know more about? What was the most difficult part of the project? What would you do differently next time?"

12. BUILD SUCCESS

Watch for opportunities to recognize success, but don't forget to note improvement, too. For example, instead of waiting for a student to master all 12 of the new spelling words, comment favorably on her having learned the first four, then encourage her to keep going.

Set up opportunities for all of your students to be successful, but be especially aware of those who may not get much positive recognition. You may want to orchestrate some success experiences for your most needy students. For example, identify something that a student does well, and plan an opportunity for him to use this skill or talent in the classroom. Small, everyday accomplishments— picking up your mail at the school office, passing out his classmates' work—can each be recognized as a job well done.

13. PROMOTE POSITIVE SELF-ESTEEM

In addition to providing your students with opportunities to be successful, incorporate other self-esteem-building strategies and activities into your curriculum. Encourage your students to express their feelings and concerns. (Find specific ideas for building student self-esteem on pages 85–86.)

Eight Teaching Pitfalls and How to Avoid Them

1. INFLEXIBLE TEACHING

A rigid approach to instruction says to students, "Learn it MY way." Given the variety of known learning styles, and the spread of learning abilities and levels within the same classroom, teaching techniques *must* be varied to give all students the opportunity to learn.

When instruction is not adjusted to individual students' needs and ways of learning, some students simply don't learn. Others, turned off by unappealing tasks, refuse to learn. Still others can't learn because they lack motivation for the task.

Inflexible teaching may also lead to power struggles. The teacher sticks to one method of teaching and learning; the student refuses to comply.

◀ ◀ ◀   *Tips for Better Teaching*

Plan a variety of activities to appeal to visual, verbal, and hands-on learners. Stay open to student ideas or revisions of your plans. Schedule projects that can be scaled up to challenge your most able students, and scaled down for your struggling students. Remember that all students need appropriate opportunities to be successful. (Find more ideas on pages 68–70.)

2. ACCEPTING POOR WORK

It's important to establish and clearly communicate your standards for student assignments and projects. After that, you must be firm in holding your students to them. Accepting "junk" may convince some of your students that this is all they are capable of doing.

◀ ◀ ◀   *Tips for Better Teaching*

Tell your students exactly what is expected of them. For example, you might say, "Your project needs to show the application of the information we learned about aerodynamics and alternative energy sources. Your transportation vehicle of the future needs to be ecologically safe. It needs to carry a minimum of two people. Your design must include a scale, must have components labeled, and must include a descriptive paragraph detailing the energy source."

Keep in mind that when you establish higher standards, some students may see you as unfair. They may balk at your expectations and even refuse to participate. Stay firm. They will come around and benefit from the experience.

3. RESCUING THE STUDENT

Some teachers rush in to rescue students from difficult learning activities. Sylvia Rimm, a psychologist who specializes in underachievement, calls this "a vote of no confidence." The student sees it as proof of her own incompetence. ("Poor kid, it's just too hard for her to understand.") Over time, she may need individual attention on a regular basis.

The student who is at the teacher's side or desk the minute an assignment is made, or who sits passively until someone helps, is a dependent child. Once the dependency pattern is in place, demanding that the child take charge may lead to confusion or refusal to work independently.

Tips for Better Teaching ▶ ▶ ▶

If a student is unsure about a question, problem, or activity, encourage him to think it through first. Have him tell you what he believes to be the solution, the process, or the answer. If he really needs help, talk him through the challenge. If it appears that he understands after all and is merely seeking attention, you may wish to limit the number of times he can request your assistance during a particular class period or school day. This will force him to sort the times when he genuinely needs help from those when he just wants attention.

4. INAPPROPRIATE EXPECTATIONS

Teachers need to establish reasonable and attainable expectations for the individual student. The student's learning goals must be ones that she can actually achieve.

Some students have been consistently told that they "should" do better. For others, expectations are so high that they become frustrated, complacent, or rebellious. On the other hand, if expectations are too low, the student may settle into comfortable mediocrity.

Tips for Better Teaching ▶ ▶ ▶

Ask yourself, "What is this child reasonably able to achieve with effort on his part?" (Find more ideas for clearly identifying appropriate learning on pages 63–66.)

5. THE NEED TO CONTROL

Some teachers need to be in charge all the time. Unfortunately, the "I am the teacher, and you will do it my way" approach simply will not work with some students. Both student and teacher may dig in, making a mutually agreed upon resolution less likely. When a war of wills is declared in the classroom, everybody loses.

Tips for Better Teaching ▶ ▶ ▶

Give your students opportunities to participate in classroom decision-making. Ask for their input in developing classroom rules of conduct and solving classroom problems and conflicts. This helps them to feel as if they're part of the team.

6. GETTING EVEN

Any teacher can become frustrated with a student's lack of interest and effort in school. Some teachers who discover that they cannot control the situation retaliate with consequences that are really ways of getting even with the student.

At the elementary school level, this may take the form of keeping students in from recess or slotting them into low-ability math or reading groups because their daily work is not getting done. At the secondary level, it may involve depriving students of the chance to participate in special projects or activities. Punishments may also include refusing to accept late work, putting students on detention, or not allowing them to take part in enrichment activities.

Punishment seldom solves the achievement problem and may make it worse. It leads to fractured relationships, loss of trust, and lessened respect on the part of both individuals.

◀ ◀ ◀ *Tips for Better Teaching*

Stay calm! Recognize that you may not be in control of some of the factors that are leading to the child's underachievement. If things you have tried in the past were unsuccessful, work with the student to figure out why. Negotiate a new plan with the student's input and commitment.

7. GIVING UP

Faced with an underachieving student and several failed strategies, some teachers just give up. Claiming that they have tried everything to no avail, it now becomes the student's responsibility to sink or swim.

◀ ◀ ◀ *Tips for Better Teaching*

Giving up on a student hardly ever has positive results. Students who have been unable to make it with a teacher's support and encouragement are not likely to make it alone. More frequently, they assume that nobody cares if they fail.

Assure the student that you know he can learn, and that you have confidence in his abilities. Point out his strengths. Decide together on an attainable goal. Start small to ensure his success. Stick with him; he needs you.

8. GETTING ANGRY

A few teachers may vent their anger through classroom put-downs or outright hostility toward troublesome students. The anger of the teacher (or any other significant adult) damages the already fragile self-esteem of the underachiever. It can also lead the student to retaliate with more frequent classroom disruptions.

Count to ten, breathe deeply, leave the room for a moment—whatever you need to do to stay calm. Remember that anger is a form of attention—negative attention, but attention nevertheless—which may be just what the student wants.

Think of positive ways to approach the student. Let her know that you care about her and her school performance, and that is why you are upset. Use "I"-statements to express your thoughts and feelings. For example, you might say something like, "I get frustrated when you don't turn in your journal assignments. You are a very fine writer, and I enjoy reading your journal entries."

Work together to resolve the conflict and tension between you. You might suggest something like, "Would it help if I gave you a copy of the journal topics for this week? You could complete the ones you missed, and maybe start to think of ideas for the rest of the week's topics."

Parents as Academic Coaches

Homes that Support Achievement

As an academic coach, you can have a profound effect on your child's learning. The environment you create at home can promote positive self-esteem and achievement, or it can foster continued academic failure, negative feelings, and lowered expectations.

How would you rate your own academic coaching abilities? How well is achievement supported in your home? Find out by completing the survey that follows. Mark items "true" if they describe your home and parenting style, "false" if they do not.

If the student lives with both parents, it's best if both complete the survey. (You can even do it together.) Keep in mind that some of the characteristics listed are positive, and some are negative.

After completing the survey, check your responses in Rating Your Home Environment on page 116.

✎ PARENT SURVEY

	TRUE	FALSE
1. We celebrate all of our child's successes and thoroughly discuss each of his failures to increase the likelihood that he will succeed in the future.	☐	☐
2. We have been careful never to speak critically about a teacher in our child's presence, nor have we taken her side against the teacher.	☐	☐
3. Both parents are in agreement about our academic expectations for our child.	☐	☐
4. When our child failed a particular subject, we excused it because one (or both) of us was not successful in that subject either.	☐	☐
5. When our child appears to be struggling with learning, we immediately assist him through the difficulty.	☐	☐
6. Our child understands that if she makes an extra effort with school work, the results are better.	☐	☐
7. We give our child incentives or rewards for school achievement.	☐	☐
8. Our child is allowed to put off his school work until late in the evening or weekend.	☐	☐
9. Our child has a regular and specific time and place to study.	☐	☐
10. Our child does not simply work until homework is done, but puts in a required amount of academic time each school day. Additional time beyond homework is used for reading, reviewing notes, and/or working on special projects or activities.	☐	☐
11. We as parents set all the rules and expectations in our home, and our child follows them.	☐	☐
12. We communicate positive, realistic, and attainable expectations to our child.	☐	☐
13. We communicate with our child clearly and effectively. Our child feels that we listen to her ideas and points of view.	☐	☐
14. Our child believes that making mistakes is a way to learn. We as parents encourage safe risk-taking.	☐	☐
15. Our child participates in activities in which success is likely with appropriate effort.	☐	☐

Eleven Positive Coaching Tips
for Parents

1. USE MODERATION

Too much celebration or analysis can lead to problems. Your child may start believing that you love him when he succeeds and criticize him when he doesn't. This attitude may encourage perfectionism.

Recognize your child's improvements, not just his successes. Help him through disappointments when things do not work out as well as he hoped. Make a strong effort to stop the roller-coaster ride of winning highs and losing lows.

2. BE POSITIVE

Be especially positive in your comments about school and your child's teachers. Listen to her complaints about school, then encourage her to see the other point of view. Ask questions like, "What do you think the teacher saw/thought/believed?" "Why do you think the teacher may want you to do that?"

If there appears to be a problem that requires your involvement, handle it in private. Make a phone call to the teacher the next day or set up a conference. Let your child know that you will follow up. However, do not allow your child to believe that you will side with her against the teacher. This may lead her to feel that she has the power in the classroom, and she may act on that feeling. At the very least, siding with the child will change the quality of the interaction between teacher and child.

3. AGREE ON AND COMMUNICATE EXPECTATIONS

It is important for your child to get the same clear message about school expectations from both Mom and Dad. If one of you shields the child from the other's expectations, the child learns to play the two of you against each other. You need to agree on what is expected of your child's academic performance.

Your standards must be appropriate for your child's abilities—neither too low nor too high. They must be in line with what your child is realistically capable of achieving. If you need help identifying reasonable academic expectations, consult your child's teacher, the school psychologist, or the school counselor.

Talk with your child about his strengths and limitations. Focus on limitations as "things you are working on," not "things you are bad at." "Working on" implies that he can and probably will improve if he puts in some time and effort. Although some of his talents and skills may never be as strong as others, improvement is always possible.

Never excuse poor performance by saying, "That's okay; I wasn't good at (math/social studies/composition/whatever) either." Treat all of your child's subjects as if they are equally important and relevant.

Up from Underachievement

4. LET THE LEARNER STRUGGLE

Your child develops feelings of confidence and competence when she is able to overcome obstacles on her own. If you rush to assist, instruct, or direct whenever things get difficult, you are sending a negative message: You are telling your child that she is not able enough, smart enough, or competent enough to figure things out for herself.

Think about how good you feel when you find your way through a difficult task. Allow your child to experience that wonderful feeling of accomplishment.

This doesn't mean that you should abandon your child to go it alone. Instead, provide support and encouragement ("I know you can figure it out"). If your child tries and still doesn't understand, coach her by talking through the problem, concept, or skill. Don't do the problem for her.

Psychologist Sylvia Rimm suggests the following assistance formula: Model the task, have your child do it once as you watch, then send her off to work on her own.

5. CONNECT EFFORT WITH RESULTS

Does your child understand that studying his spelling words during the week improves his test results on Friday? Or that proofreading an essay for English may positively influence his grade? Some children seem to think that magic rather than hard work will remedy an academic shortfall. They don't see the connection between effort and results.

When your child's effort shows improved results, call attention to this positive change. Give examples of how effort and results have worked in other areas of his life. Children seem to understand that practice improves performance in athletics and the arts, but this idea has seldom been applied to academics. Use sports or arts analogies to help your child see that effort equals improved results. For example, remind your child of how practicing the piano improved his skill in playing a particular song, or how shooting baskets at the park improved his points per game.

6. ENFORCE ACADEMIC TIME

Require your child to study in a specific place for a specific amount of time each day. Allow for some time to unwind after school, but don't let studies wait until the late evening hours. Like the rest of us, children spend time and energy worrying about what they need to do. It's often more productive just to sit down and get it done.

Some educators recommend no television until after academic time. This may, in fact, be a good incentive for your child to complete her academic time before her favorite 7:00 p.m. program begins.

Professionals seem to agree that a child will learn and concentrate better if her study area is not located in the middle of family activities. Having your child do school work in a room away from you and her siblings encourages her to be an independent learner. It also keeps you from feeling as if you need to nag her about doing her work.

Encourage your child's commitment to learning by requiring her to spend a designated amount of time each day on academic activities. Naturally, these should include required homework, but they could also include reading, reviewing notes for classes, or working on other projects related to her interests. This academic time should be spent without television, telephones, or interruptions. (Find more suggestions for academic time on pages 70–74.)

7. SHARE DECISION MAKING

How motivated and committed are you to a task you have been assigned, as compared to one where you share in the planning and decision making? Your child feels the same way. When you involve him in family plans and decisions, he feels a sense of ownership. With ownership comes a greater commitment to family rules, procedures, and practices.

For example, you might try holding family meetings on a designated day of the week. Or set them up whenever a decision needs making, or a problem needs solving. Or reserve a day or afternoon each month for a family event planned by your child. (If your family has more than one child, let them alternate in exercising this privilege.) You may wish to set geographical or financial boundaries for this event, but let the child do whatever researching and planning are necessary.

8. USE INCENTIVES

Rather than setting up negative consequences, use positive incentives to motivate your child. Keep in mind that the only incentives that work are those your child is interested in or needs. Let her determine what they will be. Steer her away from incentives based on money or material rewards. Encourage her to think about things she likes to do. For example, what about playing a game with you? Or choosing the Saturday night video and making popcorn?

Incentives should be positive, and they should be stated positively. For example, say, "If you get your math done this week, you can have a friend over this weekend," not "You *can't* have a friend over this weekend if you *don't* get your math done this week."

Incentives will need to be changed from time to time. The same rewards won't always work. And, of course, you should never provide the promised reward if the child doesn't fulfill her part of the agreement.

9. COMMUNICATE CLEARLY

Clear communication is important in developing your child's feelings of safety and security. Lawrence Greene, Director of the Developmental Learning Center in California, offers this advice on communicating effectively with your child:

▶ Use language that is understandable to the child.

▶ Recognize and appreciate the child's point of view.

▶ Be aware of the child's fears and anxieties.

- Be willing to listen to what the child has to say.

- Be sensitive to the hidden messages in the child's words.

- Recognize that particularly with adolescents, their values, attitudes, and perspectives are being influenced by others outside the family.

10. MINIMIZE ANXIETY

Your home needs to support both your child's personal and academic development. You can minimize his anxiety about learning by creating a non-threatening place for taking safe chances. Your child should feel that making a mistake will not result in criticism.

Help your child to be comfortable with both wins and losses. Recognize improvement, and be there for him in times of disappointment.

11. BUILD SELF-ESTEEM

Provide opportunities for your child to experience success. If she is caught in a failure cycle, you may need to set up a success situation. What could you ask her to do that she is almost guaranteed to complete successfully—pick up her toys, follow through on a household responsibility, run a family errand? Whatever you choose, be sure to recognize her success when she is done.

Keep in mind that it takes time to change the way one sees oneself. Especially if a child's self-esteem is low, it may be quite a while before she is completely free of the failure cycle. However, each success, no matter how small, helps to build self-esteem. Little by little, these victories add up to big changes. (Find more suggestions for boosting self-esteem on pages 85–89.)

Eight Parenting Pitfalls and How to Avoid Them

1. UNREASONABLE EXPECTATIONS

Parents need to be sure that the standards and expectations they set for their children are reasonable. Unreasonable, unattainable standards increase the likelihood of continued failure. Expectations unrelated to their wants and needs do nothing to improve motivation. Why work toward a goal they aren't interested in?

◀ ◀ ◀   *Tips for Better Parenting*

Ask yourself, "What is my child capable of, with effort on his part? What is important to him in school and for the future?" Next, think about the importance of the goal to your child. Whose goal is it, yours or his? The answers to these questions can begin a dialogue with your child that results in appropriate expectations.

2. THE NEED TO CONTROL

Some parents have a strong need to control their children, from their social life to their school performance. When a child does not do well in school, frustration can lead to an even greater need to control on the parent's part. This only escalates the parent-child conflict. Each individual pulls in the opposite direction—"You WILL" versus "I WON'T."

Tips for Better Parenting ▶ ▶ ▶

Think about which decisions for your child's safety and well-being need to be made exclusively by adults. Then think about which decisions can be shared by you and your child. Now think about which decisions can be left up to the child alone. Give your child opportunities to make and own her decisions. Also, let her live with the consequences, both positive and negative.

3. GIVING UP

Some parents get so upset with the way things are going in school that they simply give up. "We've tried, and nothing ever works, so it's your problem now," they say. The child may respond, "Then why should I care?" Chances are that the parents will witness even greater academic dives when their child perceives that their support and concern have been withdrawn.

Tips for Better Parenting ▶ ▶ ▶

Hang in there! Your child may not seem especially reasonable or even lovable in times of crisis and conflict. But he still needs to know that you're there for him.

Let him know that while you may not approve of his behavior at the moment, you are his parent and he can continue to depend on your love, support, and concern. He may not seem to want it, but he does want to know that it will be there when he decides he needs it. Tell him about your frustration, but also let him know that you are convinced that school can be different for him, and you would like to help him through those changes.

4. FREQUENT USE OF PAYOFFS

It's easy for parents to fall in the trap of using payoffs for appropriate behavior or performance. This can lead to increasingly higher demands from the child, and to a child who comes to depend on rewards. The end result is the "what-do-I-get-if-I-do-it?" mentality. If the reward is not forthcoming, the child is not likely to do what the parent requests.

Tips for Better Parenting ▶ ▶ ▶

Use positive incentives initially to get your child going. Say, "If you do this...," not "If you don't do this...." (Find more ideas for positive incentives on pages 36 and 106–107.)

5. SAVING THE CHILD

Children who are constantly being bailed out of trouble never learn their own capabilities or develop the confidence that comes from solving problems on their own. When Dad runs up to school with the forgotten lunch money, or Mom solves a math problem that the child insists is too hard, a child becomes too dependent on the parents.

Dependence can lead to a child doubting her own abilities. ("When my parents do it for me, aren't they telling me that I can't handle it? Isn't it easier to let them do it, instead of having to think for myself?")

Soon the child expects assistance with even the easiest problems. The parents tire of the child's helplessness, but they may be unable to change the dependency pattern. The child continues to manipulate the situation.

◀ ◀ ◀ *Tips for Better Parenting*

Evaluate the different situations your child encounters. In which ones might logical consequences teach a lesson? Which ones are so important that your child really needs your help?

For example, if your child is facing an assignment she says she "doesn't understand," encourage her to think it through and tell you her answers. If it's obvious that she really doesn't understand, coach her through one problem or answer. Then encourage her to work the others on her own.

6. ANGER AND GUILT TRIPS

Some parents, in frustration, fall back on threats, angry outbursts, and heavy doses of guilt when the child continues to underachieve. These tactics seldom work. The child tends either to retaliate with more anger, to get even by exerting even less effort in school, or simply to ignore the parents.

◀ ◀ ◀ *Tips for Better Parenting*

Step out of the room or away from the situation until everyone is ready to work together calmly on a new plan for change. Keep in mind that your child wants your attention, even the negative attention of your anger. Arrange to spend some special time together with the focus on having fun, not on your disappointment with his school performance.

7. PANIC

Parents who panic usually have tried unsuccessfully to change their child's behavior, or are experiencing their child's underachievement for the first time. Panic can lead to overreaction and demands to "change now." Mixed messages on "what to do about this" can result. The pressure that comes from parental panic can drive children into protecting themselves by becoming defensive or going on the offensive.

Carefully think through the situation; take your time. Is this a sudden change, or a consistent pattern of behavior? Have matters been going along smoothly until now, when your child has taken an academic dive?

Consult with your child's teacher to learn more about the reasons behind the poor academic performance. Have there been any changes in classroom routines or expectations? Has the teacher noticed any changes in your child's behavior or friendships?

Once you have put together a more complete picture of the situation, talk it over with your child. Be willing to listen to her point of view. Finally, try to decide together on a logical and reasonable course of action.

8. PUNISHMENT

Some parents use punishment in an attempt to regain control of the child and force him to make an effort in school. But what happens when everything has been taken away—telephone privileges, television, the weekend overnight—and the child is still not performing in school? Parents and children frequently end up in power struggles when punishment is used.

Tips for Better Parenting ▶ ▶ ▶

Remember that when your child walks through the door to school, he is in charge of his own achievement or lack of achievement. For this reason, he must also be involved in planning for change. Imposing a plan without his input only prolongs the power struggle. Use positive incentives rather than punishment. (Find out more about positive incentives on pages 36 and 106–107.)

THE
STRATEGY
SESSIONS

The School Review

The first step in making a plan to change a student's school performance is to discover the causes of the student's underachievement. There are several ways to gather this information. Start with the Student Self-Assessment or conduct a Student Interview. If you are a teacher, you will also want to interview the parents by telephone or in a personal conference. If you are a parent, you will want to schedule either a phone conference or a face-to-face conference with your child's teacher.

The Student Self-Assessment

▲   *Students*

This self-assessment tool serves at least two purposes. First, it helps you to recognize your own school problems. Second, it gives your coaches—your teachers and parents—valuable information to use when working with you to develop a plan for improvement.

Things don't have to be the way they are now in school. You do have some control over what happens and how you feel. School shouldn't be a place where you go to fail and feel bad about yourself. You can decide to make school a more comfortable and friendly place.

After completing the self-assessment, turn to pages 117–118. The chart on those pages will point you toward information and ideas in this book you can use to make school better for yourself.

✏ HOW WELL DO I PLAY THE SCHOOL GAME?

Check each item below that describes you and school.

_____ 1. I leave assignments and projects until the last minute.

_____ 2. In order to get something done, I may settle for less than my best.

_____ 3. If I have to choose between my school work and almost any other activity, the school work comes in second.

_____ 4. Because I am not prepared for class, I feel anxious and upset about school.

_____ 5. I worry about being embarrassed in school if the teacher calls on me and I don't know the answer.

_____ 6. I am afraid that my friends will find out that I am not doing well in school.

_____ 7. When learning seems too hard, I just give up.

_____ 8. My teachers don't seem to know or care about how I learn best.

_____ 9. I sometimes find out that I have done an assignment incorrectly because I didn't understand the directions, or because I didn't check the directions to see if I was doing it right.

_____ 10. I forget the dates that assignments are due.

_____ 11. I purposely don't do well on some assignments so my friends won't think I'm a nerd.

_____ 12. I avoid trying new things because I may not be good enough at them.

_____ 13. I kill time in class by daydreaming.

_____ 14. Sometimes I turn in my work late because I'm not satisfied with the job I did and I need more time to revise it.

_____ 15. Sometimes my teachers use words I don't understand.

_____ 16. Big projects overwhelm me. I think I'll never get them done.

_____ 17. I don't know some of the things my teachers expect me to know.

_____ 18. I have a hard time asking for help.

_____ 19. Sometimes I have so much work, I have to decide what I will and won't do. I have to take a chance on getting caught with incomplete work.

_____ 20. It doesn't matter if I work hard on an assignment or not, I never do very well.

_____ 21. Most of the time, I don't care about school.

_____ 22. I study at home just long enough to get things done.

☞

____ 23. Sometimes I get so far behind in my work that I decide to just let it go and get whatever grade they give me.

____ 24. I feel frustrated when I always have to do things the same way. Sometimes I refuse to do them at all.

____ 25. Sometimes I underestimate how long it's going to take me to get things done. Then I don't have enough time to finish, and I have to throw the work together or just skip doing it.

____ 26. I try not to be noticed in class.

____ 27. When I don't understand what's going on in class, I stop listening.

____ 28. I'm frustrated because I can't learn as quickly as some other kids.

____ 29. I never seem to study the right things for a test.

____ 30. My notes are either worthless or missing.

____ 31. I have so many things going on in my life that are more important than school. I just can't do it all.

____ 32. I have had health, drug, or alcohol problems during this school year.

____ 33. Sometimes I feel so down, I have a hard time even getting to school in the morning.

____ 34. I know I could do better if the teacher would let me do a different kind of project. I wish they would let me do it my way.

The Student Interview

To clearly identify to yourself and the student what's going on in the school game, you may choose to interview the student. Interviews should be as casual and friendly as possible. A student will not willingly share ideas, feelings, and perspectives if an adult comes across as an interrogator.

Tips for Successful Student Interviews

1. ***Try to stay positive.*** This lets the student know that you are concerned about him and want to hear what he has to say. If his responses are unrealistic, explore his point of view in a non-judgmental way. Don't just tell him that he is "wrong"; remember that he is probably expressing what he really believes to be true. Instead, ask questions that will lead him to see that there are other ways to perceive the situation. For example, you might ask, "What do you think the social studies teacher thought about the quality of your project?" This opens the door to dialogue. Introduce your questions with words such as, "What about.... What if.... What would you think, feel, or believe if...."

2. ***Avoid blaming.*** Try to focus on the issues instead of finding fault. Carefully identify the problems, describe the situation, and work together to come up with alternatives.

3. ***Practice active listening.*** Active listening involves these specific skills:

   ▶ Be patient.

   ▶ Focus on really understanding the other person's point of view.

   ▶ Stay centered on the person, not just the words he or she is saying.

   ▶ Concentrate on what the other person is saying, not on what you will say next.

   ▶ Keep the discussion going slowly enough so that both of you can truly understand what is being said.

   ▶ Think before you respond, so your comments are relevant.

   ▶ Don't be afraid to say, "Just a minute; let me think."

   ▶ Restate what you believe to be the other person's ideas or perspectives. For example: "I think you are saying that....Is that right?"

   ▶ Convey empathy, respect, and acceptance of the other person's point of view through your posture, gestures, and facial expressions as well as your words.

4. ***Don't downplay the student's perspectives and feelings.*** For example, try not to say, "You shouldn't feel that way." Validate the student's feelings by acknowledging them, then move on. For example, you might say something like, "I understand that you don't feel that your assignments are challenging enough. What would be your ideal independent project for the social studies unit?"

5. ***Don't get defensive.*** Remember that the student is presenting her point of view—her reality. If you are going to help her make a change, you need to really listen, not argue about who's right and who's wrong.

6. ***Keep your questions neutral.*** Avoid loaded words and phrases that convey your acceptance or displeasure, approval or disapproval. These may steer the student to say what you want to hear, which won't help either of you. Keeping your questions and observations neutral allows the student to express his true feelings and perspectives without getting defensive.

7. ***Give illustrations and examples whenever you can.*** For example, you might say, "Some kids have a problem getting projects in when there are many steps involved and the time line for getting them done is long. What about you? How do you feel about big projects?" Compare this to, "I hear you have a problem getting big projects done. Why is that?" Which question would you feel safer answering? The student feels the same way.

8. ***Use simulation questions to introduce other points of view.*** Try questions such as, "Why do you think your science teacher expects you to turn in your lab notebooks?" "What would you have done in that situation?" "What might be the consequences of not bringing your books to class?"

9. ***Ask for elaboration.*** Expect the student to clarify information she offers. Try questions such as, "Who was involved?" "What happened next?" "How did you feel about that?" "Can you tell me more about that?" "I don't quite understand; what else can you tell me?" "What do you specifically mean by using that word?" "Can you give me an example?"

10. ***Summarize key points.*** Go back to the main ideas or themes the student has presented and review them. You might say something like, "I think that what I'm hearing you say is....Am I right?"

11. ***Avoid solving the problem yourself.*** Let the student come up with a solution to try; that way, he will feel more committed. For example, you might ask, "What could you do in order to keep yourself from daydreaming during math class?" Then ask him to suggest some possible solutions. If necessary, help him out with ideas, such as, "Some kids find that taking notes helps them to keep listening. Other kids have tried keeping track of how many times they stop paying attention in a particular class period. Then they try to cut down on that number each day." Let the student decide which solution to put into action.

Questions for Student Interviews

Following is a preliminary list of questions for a student interview. These questions may be used by teachers and parents, since you are both trying to identify a student's school problems. Sort through the list to see which questions are appropriate for your particular student's age, grade, and circumstances. Ask those, and skip or modify the others.

The questions are grouped by problem area. As you do the interview, you should be able to begin identifying the major causes of your student's school problems, based on the responses he or she gives in each category.

LEARNING

1. What subject/class are you best in? What subject/class is the most difficult for you?

2. What do you like most about (your best subject/class)?

3. What makes (your most difficult subject/class) so hard for you?

4. What's the hardest thing for you to do: your daily work, the end-of-chapter tests, or independent projects?

5. Can you tell me what caused your grade in (the subject/class where you performed most poorly)?

6. Do you understand the material taught in (your most difficult subject/class)?

7. What school activities or projects do you enjoy the most?

8. Of all your subjects, which one do you think you could improve in? How could you improve your grade in that class?

9. If you feel you are behind in that class, do you think you could catch up? What extra help might you need?

10. What keeps you from being successful in that class? What could you do about it?

DEVELOPING STUDY HABITS

1. How much time do you typically spend each day studying or doing homework at home?

2. Do you spend a specific amount of time studying and doing homework, or do you just work until you finish your assignments?

3. Do you have a particular place where you study at home? Describe it to me.

4. Do you have a set time to begin studying each night?

5. If you need to remember something for a test, how do you memorize it?

6. Tell me about your way of taking notes.

7. Can you usually predict what might be on a test? If yes, how can you tell?

8. Do you check over your work before you turn it in?

9. Do you sometimes get distracted during your home study time? If yes, what kinds of things distract you?

10. How long can you study in one stretch? Do you give yourself a break during your study time?

11. Do you reward yourself when your study time is over?

MANAGING SCHOOL WORK

1. Are there any particular days of the week when it's more difficult to find time to study at home?

2. Is there a particular time of the school year when it's more difficult to study? (Examples: school play, athletic season.)

3. Do you keep an assignment notebook, folder, or calendar? Do you use it regularly? Does it work for you?

4. How do you organize your work for a big project that takes a long time to do? (Can you break the project down into small steps?)

5. If you have several deadlines at the same time, how do you decide what work to do each evening?

6. Each evening, when you start your study time, do you know what work needs to be done and what deadlines you have coming up?

SETTING GOALS

1. Where do you want to be and what do you want to be doing when you have completed school (or 5 to 10 years from now)?

2. What is the most important thing about school for you? What makes you (or could make you) want to come to school each day?

DEALING WITH PERSONAL ISSUES

1. If you could change one thing about yourself, what would it be?

2. What do you do to handle stress?

3. Do you believe you are a perfectionist? (Does it bother you if things are not just right? Do you have problems getting your work in on time because it doesn't seem quite finished yet? Do you ever not try something because you don't think you'll be good enough?)

The Parent Interview

To gather more information about the student, you may decide to interview the parent or parents on the telephone or schedule a personal conference. Either way, you will want to find out about the student's past school performance and any efforts that may have been made in previous years to improve school performance. You'll want to find out how willing the parents are to be involved in a cooperative plan for change. You may also want to confirm certain information the student provided in the assessment and/or interview, such as the student's study time and place at home.

Questions for Parent Interviews

Following is a preliminary list of questions for a parent interview. Sort through the list to see which questions are appropriate for the particular circumstances. Ask those, and skip or modify the others.

1. How do you feel about your child's school achievement this year (quarter)?

2. What are your concerns about (the child's) school achievement?

3. Has your child had any learning problems in the past? If yes, please tell me about them.

4. Has any subject or class been especially difficult for your child?

5. Has your child ever had any evaluation in school for learning problems?

6. What has been tried in the past to help your child learn in school? Were those plans successful or not? Why or why not?

7. Have you ever tried rewards or incentives to motivate (the child)? What has worked? What hasn't worked?

8. Does your child seem to have learning problems at a certain time of the school year, or under any particular circumstances? (NOTE: You are looking for things that compete with the student's study time, and for mismatches between how the student learns best and how learning is structured in the classroom.)

9. Has there been anything occurring lately that may be distracting (the child) from school work?

10. Does your child have a regular time and place to study at home? Please describe.

11. Does your child work well on his/her own at home, or do you need to provide reminders or supervision?

12. Are you willing to work with me and your child to improve his/her school success?

At the end of the interview: Indicate that you are concerned about the student's progress in school. Say that you would like to develop a plan for improvement. Talk with the parents about some possibilities. Try to determine whether they are willing to help you and the student develop a plan, and whether they would monitor it at home. If they are willing, arrange a meeting between you, the student, and the parents to start working out a plan. If they are not willing—not all parents will want to or be able to participate—you can still work out a plan. Be aware that this places limitations on follow-through at home. You will need to design the plan so it can be monitored, and the incentives provided, within these limitations.

The Teacher Conference

▲ *Parents*

The best way to learn more about your child's school performance is by talking with the teacher. You may do this over the telephone, but a face-to-face conference is preferable. Call the school to set up an appointment. Ask to speak to your child's teacher.

Here are three points you will want to be sure to cover when you are setting up the appointment:

▶ Tell the teacher that you are concerned about your child's achievement in school.

▶ Say that you would like to meet with the teacher to find out more about your child's school problems.

▶ Let the teacher know that you would like to set up a plan for improving your child's school performance. Explain that this plan would involve you, the teacher, and the student working together.

Giving the teacher this information in advance enables him or her to examine your child's records ahead of time and be ready with answers when you meet. You are also letting the teacher know that you are coming in as a concerned parent who is willing to help, not as an angry adversary.

Questions for
Teacher Conferences

Following is a preliminary list of questions to assist you in planning for your teacher conference. Sort through the list to see which questions are appropriate for your particular circumstances. Ask those, and skip or modify the others.

1. What seems to be the cause of my child's grade in (a problem class)? (For example, is the issue daily work? Test scores? Some other factor?)

2. Does my child have the capability to be in this class? Does my child have the basic skills necessary to be successful in this class?

3. Does my child have the capability to do more advanced work than the other students in this class?

4. Does he/she ask for help in class?

5. Does he/she appear to be paying attention in class?

6. Are there circumstances in the class that may be distracting him/her? (For example, does your child sit next to a best friend?)

7. Does he/she participate in class discussions and activities?

8. Is his/her work turned in on time?

9. Does my child follow your directions for class activities and written work?

10. What are your expectations for the children in your class this year?

11. Do your students typically have time in class to work on homework and other assignments?

12. Do your students get written instructions for major projects?

13. Are your students reminded of deadlines? How?

14. Do your students understand how they will be graded? (What are the criteria for grades? What are the teacher's standards?)

15. What might my child do to improve his/her grades and learning in your class?

At the end of the conference: Indicate that you would like to make a plan for improvement. Try to determine whether the teacher is willing to participate in developing the plan and monitoring it at school. If the teacher is interested in working with you, make arrangements to meet with the teacher and your child to start developing a plan. If the teacher is not interested—most will be, but some may not be—you can still work out a plan. Be aware that this places limitations on follow-through at school. You will need to design the plan so it can be monitored, and the incentives provided, within these limitations.

The Action Plan
Action Plan Part A:
The Academic Profile

Once you have gathered information about the student's abilities and school performance, you're ready to decide what you can reasonably expect from the student. The following ideas may be used by teachers and parents, since you are both concerned with finding a match between the student's abilities and your expectations for his or her school performance.

STEP 1: REVIEW THE STUDENT'S STANDARDIZED TEST SCORES

Look in particular at aptitude and achievement test information, if available.

▶ *Aptitude test scores* give you an idea of the student's natural abilities in up to three areas: *verbal, quantitative* (math), and *nonverbal* or *spatial* (abstract thinking).

Scores are typically reported as percentiles. They may compare the student to others in the nation (national percentile), or to others in your school district (local percentile).

The *verbal score* reflects the student's knowledge and understanding of words. It gives you an indication of her performance potential in such areas as reading and language arts.

The *quantitative score* summarizes the student's mathematical thinking abilities. It can help you to predict his possible performance in mathematics.

The *nonverbal* or *spatial score* relates more to the student's abstract thinking abilities. These skills may reflect her ability to make mental pictures, or to do geometry.

It is not uncommon for students to score higher in one area and lower in the others. In most cases, this simply indicates a mental preference for a certain kind of learning—verbal, mathematical, or visual.

▶ *Achievement test scores* reflect how well the student has learned the information presented in school. The scores measure and compare his learning to that of others at the same grade level. The questions and activities in the assessments are designed to represent typical learning for each grade level.

Percentile scores are usually available. As with aptitude testing, these scores may indicate a national or local comparison. Scores are available for mathematics, reading, language arts, social studies, and science, as well as such areas as work/study skills and reference skills.

Not all school districts give all of the assessments, and schools tend to choose the scores they believe will be most helpful for curriculum planning and evaluating student progress. Still, achievement test scores can give you a reasonable indication of how a particular student is progressing compared to other students in his grade.

STEP 2: TALK WITH THE TEACHERS

If you are a parent, plan a conference with your child's teachers to learn their perspectives on her abilities. What do they see as her strengths and needs?

If you are a teacher, talk with other teachers who have had the student in previous grades or subjects. What did they see as her strengths and limitations?

STEP 3: COMPARE PREDICTED PERFORMANCE AND GRADES

As you review available test scores and information from teachers, keep the student's grades in mind. Do they adequately reflect what his predicted performance would be in each subject? (Find out how to determine appropriate expectations on page 64.)

For example, high verbal aptitude and language arts achievement scores, combined with teacher reports of the student's advanced reading and speaking abilities, might lead you to predict high grades in language arts class. If, in fact, the student's grades are average or low-average, something is wrong. *Discrepancies between predicted performance and grades are red flags for underachievement.*

Or maybe the student's test scores are not high, but his teachers describe him as bright and capable—someone whose scores should be higher. Remember that lack of effort leads to lack of learning, and over time, this lowers achievement test scores. The student still has the ability to learn. He has simply stopped learning.

STEP 4: USE THE INFORMATION YOU HAVE GATHERED TO COMPLETE ACTION PLAN PART A: THE ACADEMIC PROFILE

The Academic Profile that follows is a tool that will help you to clearly describe the student's abilities and determine reasonable expectations for her school performance.

To complete the Academic Profile:

a. Under the Abilities section, enter the student's national percentile scores for each subject given in the achievement tests.

b. Enter the student's final grades in these subjects for the past three years.

c. Enter the student's current quarterly grades for each of the subjects.

d. Enter the student's national percentile scores in aptitude testing.

e. Enter the results of intelligence testing information, if available.

f. Using the process described on page 64, predict the student's performance in terms of grades that could be attained with effort on the student's part. Enter these grades in the Predicted Performance section of the Academic Profile.

✎ ACADEMIC PROFILE

Student's Name _____ Grade _____ School _____

Parents _____

Address _____

Telephone (home) _____ Mother (work) _____

Father (work) _____

Homeroom Teacher _____

ABILITIES:

ACHIEVEMENT			FINAL GRADES			CURRENT GRADES		
Subject	National %		Yr 1	Yr 2	Yr 3	1	2	3

APTITUDE	NATIONAL %
Verbal	
Quantitative	
Nonverbal (Spatial)	

PREDICTED PERFORMANCE (GRADES):

Reading _____

Language Arts _____

Social Studies _____

Science _____

Mathematics _____

INTELLIGENCE TESTING: _____

ADDITIONAL COMMENTS: _____

_____

_____

_____

_____

_____

Action Plan Part B:
The Problem Checklist

When you have completed the Academic Profile, you are ready to start identifying the student's problem areas. The Problem Checklist on pages 57–59 is a convenient format for doing this. The Checklist also points you toward specific suggestions for working on the problems you identify.

Before you complete the Checklist, you may find it helpful to consult the Players' Prescriptives chart that follows. The chart identifies typical problem areas for each of the underachievers profiled earlier, on pages 12–20.

Think about your student and review the profiles. Does your student resemble one of these? For example, let's say your student sounds like the Distracted Learner described on page 17. Looking at the Players' Prescriptives chart, you see that the Distracted Learner typically has five major problem areas: managing work, setting goals, friends, stress, and health issues. You might keep these in mind as you complete the Problem Checklist.

Of course, it is also possible for a student to exhibit a blend of several profile characteristics. The Prescriptives are not meant to be the last word on any student, including yours. Rather, they are intended as one more source of information to consult as you try to understand your student's problems and needs.

Information gathered through the Student Self-Assessment, the Student Interview, the Parent Interview, and/or the Teacher Conference will also guide your completion of the Problem Checklist.

PLAYERS' PRESCRIPTIVES

	MAJOR PROBLEM AREAS											
	LEARNING						PERSONAL ISSUES					
	Appropriate Learning	Value for Learning	Learning Style	Study Habits	Managing Work	Setting Goals	Self-Esteem	Perfectionism	Friends	Stress	Power and Control	Health Issues
REBEL	X	X				X					X	
CONFORMIST	X						X		X			
STRESSED					X	X		X		X		
STRUGGLING	X		X	X	X		X			X		
VICTIM				X	X						X	
DISTRACTED					X	X			X	X		X
BORED	X		X									
COMPLACENT						X					X	
SINGLE-SIDED	X	X	X		X							

✎ PROBLEM CHECKLIST

Check the items below that you believe contribute to your student's lack of school success. Items are grouped by problem area. The sections referenced in the right-hand column point you toward ideas in Success Boosters (pages 61–101) appropriate for working on your student's specific problems.

I. LEARNING (pages 63–70)

THE STUDENT: **SEE:**

_____ 1. Does not see the importance of classroom learning.   Developing a Value for Learning, pages 66–68

_____ 2. Is involved in learning that does not provide enough challenge. Identifying Appropriate Learning, pages 63–66

_____ 3. Is involved in learning that is too difficult.   Identifying Appropriate Learning, pages 63–66

_____ 4. Lacks the basic skills needed to be successful.   Identifying Appropriate Learning, pages 63–66

_____ 5. Has learning disabilities or deficits that affect the ability to learn. Identifying Appropriate Learning, pages 63–66

_____ 6. Gives up when learning becomes too hard.   Identifying Appropriate Learning, pages 63–66

_____ 7. Daydreams; does not listen attentively in class.   Identifying Appropriate Learning, pages 63–66

_____ 8. Refuses to participate in class discussions or activities.   Developing a Value for Learning, pages 66–68
Identifying Learning Style, pages 68–70

_____ 9. Is passive in the classroom, shows little involvement in or enthusiasm for learning. Developing a Value for Learning, pages 66–68
Identifying Learning Style, pages 68–70

_____ 10. Challenges or refuses to do assignments because of "boredom." Identifying Appropriate Learning, pages 63–66

_____ 11. Is distracted during learning.   Identifying Appropriate Learning, pages 63–66
Identifying Learning Style, pages 68–70

_____ 12. Refuses to complete assignments or decides to just let them go. Developing a Value for Learning, pages 66–68

_____ 13. Does just enough to get by.   Developing a Value for Learning, pages 66–68

_____ 14. Is not motivated by class activities and projects.   Identifying Learning Style, pages 68–70

_____ 15. Lacks a goal for school achievement.   Developing a Value for Learning, pages 66–68

_____ 16. Does not see a need for school in his or her future plans.   Developing a Value for Learning, pages 66–68

_____ 17. Lacks role models for achievement.   Developing a Value for Learning, pages 66–68

_____ 18. Other: _____

II. DEVELOPING STUDY HABITS (pages 70–78)

THE STUDENT:

_____ 1. Does not proofread or check over work.

_____ 2. Does not put in sufficient time to produce quality work.

_____ 3. Does not have a study method to help remember information.

_____ 4. Does not have a regular schedule and time commitment for study.

_____ 5. Does not have an efficient and effective way to take notes.

_____ 6. Cannot predict possible items in an exam; cannot separate important from unimportant information.

_____ 7. Lacks a place to study away from distractions.

_____ 8. Has competition for study time (is overcommitted).

_____ 9. Other: _____

III. MANAGING SCHOOL WORK (pages 78–79)

THE STUDENT:

_____ 1. Does not have a method for keeping track of assignments and deadlines.

_____ 2. Does not know how to break down a large project into small, accomplishable steps.

_____ 3. Leaves work until the last minute.

_____ 4. Does not successfully prioritize activities when several things need to be done.

_____ 5. Other: _____

IV. SETTING GOALS (pages 79–84)

THE STUDENT:

_____ 1. Does not know how to set long-term or short-term goals.

_____ 2. Lacks appropriate incentives for school performance.

_____ 3. Cannot identify obstacles to progress or find ways to overcome them.

_____ 4. Does not see the benefits of change.

_____ 5. Lacks home or school support for change.

_____ 6. Other: _____

V. DEALING WITH PERSONAL ISSUES (pages 85–101)

THE STUDENT: **SEE:**

_____ 1. Has pressure from friends not to do too well.   Friends, pages 93–97

_____ 2. Has low self-esteem; does not believe it is possible to succeed.   Self-Esteem, pages 85–89

_____ 3. Is in a power struggle at home or school.   Power and Control, page 99

_____ 4. Lacks respect for the teacher and/or parent.   Power and Control, page 99

_____ 5. Is a perfectionist who can't settle for less than the best; may fail to turn in work even when it is complete because it isn't yet "good enough."   Perfectionism, pages 89–93

_____ 6. Has unrealistic expectations (either too high or low) set by self, parent, or teacher.   Perfectionism, pages 89–93

_____ 7. Is stressed and anxious.   Stress, pages 97–98

_____ 8. Lacks confidence in his or her academic skills.   Self-Esteem, pages 85–89

_____ 9. Is a poor risk taker (not willing to try new activities).   Perfectionism, pages 89–93

_____ 10. Does not recognize personal improvement, only being "the best."   Perfectionism, pages 89–93

_____ 11. Has family problems (examples: divorce, move to a new city, other change in living situation).   Stress, pages 97–98

_____ 12. Has health problems (examples: long illness, eating disorder).   Health, pages 100–101

_____ 13. Has alcohol or other chemical dependency problems.   Health, pages 100–101

_____ 14. Has mental health problems (example: depression).   Health, pages 100–101

_____ 15. Other: _____

SUCCESS
BOOSTERS

What Are Success Boosters?

Success Boosters are specific strategies you can use to help your student with his or her school problems. They also include ideas that students can use to help themselves.

Pay special attention to those that relate to your student's school problems, as identified in the Players' Prescriptives (page 56) and the Problem Checklist (pages 57–59).

The First Step:
Breaking the Failure Cycle

Breaking a student's cycle of failure is the easiest way to start changing his motivation and achievement in school.

A student who has become caught in a never-ending cycle of school failure suffers a downward spiral of self-esteem. Children who have negative feelings about themselves lack motivation. In the school setting, lack of motivation to learn leads to more failure, reinforcing their feelings that they can't learn. Such negative feelings can only lead to more failure.

Teachers and parents must recognize that change occurs in small steps. If you attempt to address all problem areas immediately and simultaneously, you and the student will fail. Instead, plan small steps. Focus on one area at a time, so the student is not overwhelmed by all that needs to be done. Discuss a goal and reach agreement on a plan. Set up a time line of a few weeks (typically 2–4 weeks) to really work on this problem. Check progress frequently.

▶ For students in grades 1–3, progress should be checked *daily.*

▶ Older students in grades 4–12 should have *weekly* progress checks.

If a particular strategy isn't working for you, go back and review the situation again. Talk it over with your student, and come up with a new strategy to try.

Breaking a failure cycle takes persistence, patience, and time. Plan opportunities for success, get your student involved, and watch success bump his self-esteem in positive directions. Once he begins expecting success instead of failure, each positive experience will move him toward greater motivation to learn.

▲ Teachers

▶ *Think of classroom tasks the student can complete successfully.* For example, handing out materials for an art activity, returning a film to the school media specialist, or setting up a science experiment are often tasks given to those who finish first or are seen as responsible class members. In many classrooms, those who are last and late seldom get to perform these simple responsibilities. Turn them into success experiences for the underachiever.

▶ *Break down class assignments into small steps, with checkpoints along the way.* This will enable the student to experience the success of completion several times, not only when she hands in the final project. Provide plenty of praise for meeting the deadlines.

▶ *Watch for opportunities to notice positive efforts.* Whether this involves commenting on a fine idea on a not-so-neat essay, or mentioning improvement in the number correct on a math assignment, reinforce steps toward success when you see them.

Parents ▲

▶ *Look for opportunities around the home to build successes.* Recognize and acknowledge such activities as straightening a messy room, loading the dishwasher correctly, arranging an overnight with friends, and caring for the family pet. If you want your child's performance to meet your standards, remember to explain in detail what needs to be done.

▶ *Select activities in the home or community that may provide success experiences.* For example, after-school or summer classes chosen by your child and taken just for fun can be very positive. If he is interested, sports activities such as soccer, or an after-school activity such as chess club, can provide other opportunities for success that are not school-based. Think about his interests, and look for ways to turn his passions into chances for success.

Learning

Identifying Appropriate Learning (Is School Too Easy for the Student, or Too Hard?)

Teachers and Parents ▲

A too-easy curriculum is as unmotivating as a curriculum which is beyond the student's grasp. Learning needs to be challenging, but not unattainable. It needs to assure success without being repetitive and redundant. And it needs to motivate, not overwhelm.

For all this to happen, there must be a match between the student's abilities and aptitudes and her learning goals. Following are guidelines to help you arrive at such a match.

1. DETERMINE APPROPRIATE EXPECTATIONS

Students whose test scores are in the top percentiles (mid to high 90's) need learning that is appropriately advanced and accelerated. Repeating information and practicing skills that have already been mastered can lead to laziness, boredom, sloppy work, or even rebellion and refusal to participate.

Strong aptitude and achievement (80's and 90's) in a particular subject should predict high performance—work at the A or B level. Keep in mind, however, that interest is often a motivator. If a student is not interested in a particular subject, his grades may not be as high as we might like them to be, regardless of his high potential. Often, this is just fine.

Students of average to high-average aptitude and achievement (60's to 80's) in a particular subject should be expected to perform at an average or high-average level—B or C level work. Keep in mind that some students with average potential have high interest in a particular subject and work hard to learn it. These students may also become A students.

If your student has learning disabilities or differences, find out what assistance is available to help him overcome or cope with these obstacles.

Tip ▶ ▶ ▶

Look for a match between your student's needs and abilities and the learning being provided in the classroom. Are the learning activities challenging enough to interest your highest ability student? Is the less able student likely to be successful with adequate effort?

2. ESTABLISH STANDARDS FOR SCHOOL PERFORMANCE AND EFFORT

It is important to clearly and precisely describe the standards for school performance and effort. For example, it is not enough for the student to make a commitment "to study at home." Your agreement must specify *when, where,* and *for how long* the student will study at home.

Define and agree on what you all mean by "appropriate effort." For example, it is not enough to say that the student "will complete daily math work." Your agreement must specify that she will complete daily math work for four out of five days (particularly if the pattern in the past has been two out of five days). It is more realistic to raise expectations for school performance and effort gradually, rather than demanding a 100-percent turnaround overnight.

Tip ▶ ▶ ▶

Be specific in terms of what is expected, and clearly communicate these expectations to the student. Keep in mind these standards for school performance and your agreed-upon definition of appropriate effort as you complete Action Plan Part C: The Commitment to Action with your student.

3. MEET TO COMMUNICATE IDEAS AND DECISIONS

Academic coaches—teachers and parents—should meet to share their ideas for learning plans. Preferably, the student should be there, too, so everyone has a chance to participate and reach an agreement. Don't be afraid to frankly discuss the student's strengths and limitations in his presence. Make sure to give the student an opportunity to share his ideas and viewpoints.

◀ ◀ ◀ *Tip*

For real change to take place, all members of the team—parents, teachers, and student—need to understand, agree with, and commit to the plan for change. If there is any disagreement, the plan should be renegotiated until everyone feels comfortable with it.

Students ▲

IF YOUR WORK IS TOO EASY

1. Think about what else you would like to learn about in that subject or unit.

2. Think about a project or activity you would like to do. Write down your ideas.

3. Ask your teachers if there is a time before or after school when you can talk to them. Make an appointment to meet.

4. At that meeting, tell your teachers what you would like to learn more about. Explain why this topic is especially interesting to you.

   Be respectful, and choose your words carefully. You do not want your teachers to think that you are criticizing their teaching ideas. Use "I"-statements to get your message and feelings across. For example, you might say things like, "I would like to know more about...." "I am interested in...." "I am curious about...because...."

5. Ask your teachers if you can show them that you know the basic material. Here are some ideas to suggest:

   ▶ You could take the test early.

   ▶ You could work through the required material on your own.

   ▶ You could skip some of the basic material you already know and do an advanced project or activity instead.

6. Be ready with a plan. Suggest your ideas for the project or activity you would like to do. Show or tell your teachers the ideas you wrote down. Be ready to listen to their ideas and accept possible revisions to your plan.

7. Decide together what your project or activity will be, and when you will have class time to work on it.

IF YOUR WORK IS TOO HARD

1. Think about what is making the subject or unit so difficult for you. Do you understand the information? Are there skills or information your teachers expect you to know that you don't know? Are the assignments too difficult for you? What makes them difficult? *Be specific about the problems you are having in that subject or unit.*

2. Are there things you could do to be more successful in that subject or unit? Write down your ideas. For example, if you're working on a research paper, maybe you could break it down into small steps—notes, outline, rough draft, final draft—and turn in each step as you finish it, at a time your teachers determine. Or perhaps you could use a tape recorder to help you take notes in class.

3. Ask your teachers if there is a time before or after school when you can talk to them. Make an appointment to meet.

4. At that meeting, tell your teachers what you believe makes the subject or unit too hard for you. Be respectful, and choose your words carefully. Express concern without criticizing. Use "I"-statements to get your message and feelings across. For example, you might say things like, "I don't understand...." "I think it is hard for me to...." "I have trouble with...."

5. Be ready to share your ideas about how you could be more successful. Ask your teachers for more ideas.

6. Decide together what ideas you will try. Remember that your teachers want you to succeed.

Developing a Value for Learning (Is Learning Important to the Student?)

For the student to be motivated to learn, she needs to believe that learning is important. Throughout this book, there are ideas and suggestions that can help you convey that learning matters. For example, when you show the student how learning applies to the real world, you let her know that specific information and skills have real meaning and value.

Jere Brophy, a professor of education at Michigan State University, offers the following guidelines for communicating the importance of learning.

▲ Parents

▶ *Model.* Show your value for and enthusiasm toward learning. Share what you find interesting or intriguing about a topic. Comment on an article in a newspaper or magazine, or remark on a television program or news broadcast. Say things like, "I remember...," "I read...," "I heard..." to open up a discussion with your child.

► **Communicate.** Capture any moments that become available to become actively involved in educating your child. Discuss new topics as he expresses interest or curiosity, but don't lecture him on the topics. Elaborate on ideas. Pose open-ended questions.

For example, in standing in front of a museum display of predatory birds, don't just tell him about the talons and their uses. Ask questions like, "How do you think that bird uses talons? How is this bird different from the one on the other side of the display? How is it similar?" Questions get your child curious and involved. They also let him know that you are learning along with him.

► **Make learning a pleasure.** Be aware of opportunities within your community where your child can experience the joy of learning for its own sake. Look for community education offerings and programs at local museums or college campuses. Develop your own home learning experiences. Base these activities on your child's strongest interests.

Teachers ▲

► **Model.** Tell your students what excites, interests, or intrigues you about a subject, topic, or issue. Weave your personal experiences, perspectives, and ideas into your lesson plans. Give your students opportunities to share what they know about a topic. Enthusiasm can be contagious.

► **Communicate.** Let your students know that you value their learning and their efforts to learn. Show them through your words and actions. Tell them that you want them to be curious, to ask questions, to request explanations, and to get excited about new information. Be flexible; if your students get intensely involved in a topic or activity, don't cut them off just because the clock or your lesson plan book says it's time to move on.

► **Make learning a pleasure.** Provide learning experiences that get your students curious, interested, and actively involved. Limit the passive learning in your classroom. Find alternatives to the teacher-talking-in-the-front-of-the-room, students-listening-at-their-desks routine.

Plan learning activities that grab your students' attention and spark their enthusiasm. Be a judge of your own lesson plans by asking yourself, "Would I like to do this? Would I find this fun, challenging? Would I feel involved?"

Students ▲

► **Read about or talk to interesting and successful people.** Try to find some people who have jobs or careers that you might like to try in the future. Interview them or start up a conversation about their work. What kind of schooling did they have? What experiences in their lives helped them to become successful?

▶ *Interview or spend time with people who have interests, hobbies, or jobs that you believe are important.* What skills do they use in their work or play? What do they need to know to do well? For example, if you think you might want to work as a sportscaster or a horse trainer someday, or if you would like to be great on the guitar, find out what it would take to realize your dream.

Identifying Learning Style (How Does the Student Learn Best?)

▲ Teachers, Parents and Students

Not everyone learns in the same way. The different ways people learn are called their *learning styles*. Learning styles are important because learning becomes more difficult when styles and teaching methods clash.

The learning setting can either support or frustrate the individual's learning style. For example, the student who learns best through hands-on experiences will not learn as much from a lecture class. Some students can learn about a subject by reading; others need pictures, maps, and graphs before they can truly understand the material.

A good way to understand learning styles is by finding out about your own. The following survey is designed for anyone who wants to know about his or her learning style—parents, teachers, and students. It might be fun if all of you complete this survey and share your results. If that isn't possible, consider having the student complete the survey. Add the results to other information being gathered about the student, and keep them in mind as you work together on Action Plan Part C: The Commitment to Action.

✎ LEARNING STYLE SURVEY

Check the words and phrases that describe how you like to learn.

1. **When are you most ready to learn?**

   ____ in the morning

   ____ in the afternoon

2. **What is your favorite way to learn?**

   ____ on my own

   ____ one-to-one with an adult (teacher, parent, mentor)

   ____ one-to-one with a friend or classmate

   ____ in a small group

   ____ in a medium-size group

   ____ in a large group (with the whole class)

3. **Where is your favorite place to learn?**

   ____ in a classroom with other people

   ____ off by myself somewhere, away from other people

   ____ in a small study area

   ____ in a library

4. **When you are doing an activity, can you stick with it for...**

   ____ a long period of time?

   ____ a short period of time?

5. **How do you learn best?**

   ____ by reading books, articles, and other printed materials

   ____ by looking at maps, pictures, or charts, and by watching demonstrations

   ____ by listening

   ____ by doing things with my hands (examples: drawing, working with objects, doing experiments, making things, building things)

6. **When you are learning...**

   ____ can you tell on your own how well you are doing? Or...

   ____ do you need someone else to tell you if you are on the right track?

7. **When you are learning...**

   ____ do you learn the parts first, then understand the whole idea? Or...

   ____ do you need to see the whole, completed idea first, then learn the details?

8. **Which would you rather do?**

   ____ use facts and information to do practical projects

   ____ gather information, analyze ideas, and write essays about what you are learning

   ____ use facts and information to do a group project

   ____ discover new information and ideas, then create your own new answers or products

9. **Which way do you learn most easily?**

   ____ with exact directions and examples

   ____ with lecture notes and written materials

   ____ by working and sharing with others

   ____ by solving problems and trying new approaches

USING INFORMATION ABOUT LEARNING STYLES

Working together, teachers, parents, and students can set the stage for the best possible learning situation. Discussions about learning style needs can help make it happen. The more frequent the match between the learning activity and the learner's style, the greater the likelihood that the student will be motivated by the activity.

For example, secondary school students who learn best in the morning can try to schedule their toughest classes for early in the day. Teachers can give students a choice of projects that respect various learning styles. Students who learn best by hearing information can use tape recorders to "take notes" during class lectures. Parents whose children learn best with others can organize after-school study groups.

There are many possibilities to explore, and many ideas to try. For all students—and especially for those who underachieve—an awareness of learning styles, and more opportunities to learn in their preferred style, can make a big difference in improving school motivation and performance.

▲ ▲ ▲ ▲

To find out more about learning styles, read:
It's All in Your Mind: A Student's Guide to Learning Style *by Kathleen Butler, Ph.D. (Columbia, CT: Learner's Dimension, 1988). Also available:* A Teacher's Guide for It's All in Your Mind.
Learning and Teaching Style: In Theory and Practice *by Kathleen Butler, Ph.D. (Columbia, CT: Learner's Dimension, 1986).*

Developing Study Habits

Since academic time is "home time," this section focuses primarily on information for parents and students. However, teachers may want to share these tried-and-true guidelines as they provide advice and assistance to parents on setting up a home study routine.

The Space

Most experts agree that the best place to study is away from possible distractions—meaning not in the middle of the living room near the television and family activities, and not at the kitchen table near the telephone.

▶ Find a spot that can become permanent, so it becomes associated with school work. It should be located away from family noise and possible interruptions.

▶ Choose an area that is comfortable and well lit.

▶ Choose appropriate furniture: a desk or table with enough room to spread out books, papers, and other learning materials; a straight-backed chair of the right height (the student should be able to place both feet flat on the floor).

▶ Equip the home study space with everything the student will need to work: pens, pencils, eraser, pencil sharpener, stapler, paper clips, markers, lined and unlined paper, dictionary, ruler, graph paper, and other supplies required for special projects.

The Schedule

It is important to establish a *reasonable and regular* study schedule. Here is what the experts recommend for academic times and frequencies:

Grade	How Long	How Often
Preschool through grade 1	10–15 minutes	3 days a week
Grades 2–3	10–20 minutes	5 days a week
Grades 4–6	20–30 minutes	5 days a week
Grades 7–9	45–60 minutes	5–6 days a week
Grades 10–12	2–3 hours	5–6 days a week

The student may spend the academic time for Day 5 or 6 anytime during the weekend.

▶ *Anticipate possible distractions such as telephone calls or friends stopping over to see your child.* Answer the phone yourself and take messages, or use an answering machine during academic time. Encourage your child to tell her friends to call after her academic time. Communicate and stand firm on your academic time policy: No interruptions allowed!

▶ *Initially, monitor your child to make sure he is spending his academic time on the right things*—homework, reading, reviewing notes, working on school-related projects or activities. Monitoring doesn't mean sitting with your child. It should be enough to walk past the room now and then to look in on how things are going. If your child is refusing to go along with the schedule, feel free to extend his time equal to the "wasted minutes." As academic time becomes part of everyday life in your household, monitoring should no longer be necessary.

▲ Students

▶ *Look at your weekly commitments to help you decide when to schedule your academic times.* For example, if you have soccer on Tuesdays and Thursdays until 5:00 p.m., you will need to study after dinner rather than right after school. Set up a weekly plan that fits with your school, athletic, club, and work commitments. You'll find a sample plan on pages 121–122.

Tip ▶ ▶ ▶

Get in the habit of completing your weekly plan by Sunday evening. Post it to remind yourself and your family of your commitments for the week. (This can also help your parents by letting them know your transportation needs and any potential conflicts during the week.)

▶ *Avoid distractions by planning ahead.* For example, let your friends know about your study schedule, and tell them to call or stop by after your academic time is up. Ask a family member to grab the phone during that time and let your friends know when you can call them back, or use an answering machine.

Tip ▶ ▶ ▶

Let your friends be your reward for honoring your academic time. Call them or get together after your time commitment is fulfilled.

What to Study

▲ Parents

▶ *Your child must use all of his required academic time for academic work.* This will discourage him from rushing through assignments if he usually only "studies" until the work is done. It will also encourage him to check over or revise his work, since he has to stay there anyway until his academic time is up.

Naturally, this doesn't mean that your child should work *only* until the academic time is over. If his work is not complete, he is not through studying.

▶ *If your child finishes her assigned work early, she should fill the rest of the time with other academic activities.* For example, she might review class notes or textbook reading, do additional reading on the topic, read for pleasure on a special topic that may or may not be used for extra credit, or work on a hobby with an academic bent (in other words, not her rock music collection).

◂ ◂ ◂ *Tip*

Work with your child to make a list of possible activities she could do in her spare academic time. These should fit general "academic" guidelines—they may be either related to what she is learning in school, or other things she simply wants to know more about. Have all necessary supplies, materials, and resources ready and at hand.

Teachers ▲

▶ **Communicate your homework policy and practice to parents and students early in the year.** For example, do you regularly assign work meant to be done at home, or do your students only bring home work that has not been completed in class? Do your students have special projects or activities that require substantial work at home? What, in your mind, is a typical amount of time your students need to spend each day or week in preparation for your class?

◂ ◂ ◂ *Tip*

Send a letter home at the beginning of each semester, quarter, or unit, laying out the plan for the coming weeks.

▶ **Provide your students with a weekly or monthly course syllabus or outline.** Spell out the content of the unit or chapter and the flow of reading assignments, writing assignments, and related projects. This will help your students to determine what they need to work on and when. (Find more suggestions on pages 78–79.)

▶ **Plan a study guide for reading assignments that lets your students know what to notice as they read.** List several questions for them to think about as they read. Include questions that ask them to compare, contrast, and/or evaluate the information. You might also ask your students to come up with new ideas or make future predictions based on what they read. A study guide will teach your students to identify what is important in their reading.

▶ **Provide written criteria for all major projects and activities.** Describe the specific content you expect to see in the final project, and the exact format the project should follow. For example, if you are studying the states, you might assign "travel brochures" for selected states. You might decide that each brochure should include information on the state's geography, climate, major waterways, cities, and points of interest. You might decide that the format should be color, illustrated with drawings or photographs, and able to fit into a business-size envelope. Put these criteria in writing for your students. The quality of their projects will improve if they know in advance what you expect.

▶ ***Provide a list of recommended or supplemental readings.*** Choose books, magazines, and other resources that are likely to be of interest and help to your students.

Tip ▶ ▶ ▶

For each unit or topic, have the students contribute ideas for a "read-more-about-it" list.

▶ ***Provide a list of possible projects or activities your students may choose to do at home, during academic time.*** Suggest a wide variety of tasks that require different amounts of time and effort to complete; these should range from quick to comprehensive. Come up with choices sensitive to the different ways your students prefer to learn and present information. You may not get many takers, but the ideas will be there for those who want to go further or earn extra points or credit.

Tip ▶ ▶ ▶

Have your students generate a list of possible projects or activities. Make copies of the list and hand them out in class.

▲ Students

▶ ***Make a daily list of what needs to get done during your academic time.*** Remember to tackle the most difficult work first. Check things off as you finish them (this feels great!). You will find sample work plans on pages 121–126.

▶ ***Schedule a break during your academic time.*** Your break should be no longer than ten minutes. Remember that this is added to your academic time, not subtracted from it.

Choose a time to take your break based on your ability to concentrate. Is it best for you to split your time exactly in half? Or is it better to take your break toward the end of your academic time, when the tough work is done? Only you know how long you can work effectively.

Plan a mini-reward during your break—a healthful snack, a jog around the block, or a quick chat with a parent or sibling.

▶ ***Plan ahead for extra activities to do if you finish your regular work early.*** Is there a project coming up that you could start working on? Is there some reading you could begin early? Have you asked your teacher about extra projects you might do, or discussed ideas for special work? What's your most difficult subject—can you review your notes or your text to better understand the material?

Tip ▶ ▶ ▶

Keep a list in your study area of projects or activities that are coming up, or extra activities you might like to do. Add to your list as you have new and interesting ideas.

The Essentials

Competent note-taking and proofreading are critical for improving and maintaining school success. This is especially true as students advance through the grades, and content and skills become more difficult.

Students ▲

FIVE TIPS ON TAKING NOTES DURING CLASS LECTURES

1. Listen for the major points your teachers make. They may emphasize these by their tone of voice, by writing information on the board or overhead projector, by repeating ideas more than once, or even by saying, "This is important!"

2. Write down the major points in your own words.

3. Listen for details. Write them down, along with examples that will help you to understand the information you are hearing.

4. Use symbols or abbreviations to help speed your note taking. Draw pictures or sketches if they help you remember the information.

5. Highlight the most important information. Use arrows or stars, circles or underline. Important information would include key words, phrases, definitions, and dates.

FIVE TIPS ON TAKING NOTES FROM READING ASSIGNMENTS

1. First, scan the pages of your reading assignment. Notice any illustrations, maps, charts, or graphs. Look for **bold print** or *italics*, which are often used to point out important information. "Previewing" your reading assignment will give you an idea of what you will be learning about.

2. Next, read the end-of-chapter or unit questions (if there are any). These will clue you in to what to look for as you read.

3. Now read each paragraph, and write down one sentence in your own words that summarizes what you read. Include main points and enough details to help you understand what you just read.

4. Add important details to your notes by reading and studying all graphs, charts, maps, diagrams, or illustrations.

5. Reread the end-of-chapter or unit questions. Look back at your notes. Do your notes answer or help you to answer these questions? If not, go back and add any important information you left out the first time around.

PROOFREADING

Before you turn in your work, take the time to check it over. Try these three tips:

1. *Make sure that you have completed the right assignment, and that you have done it correctly.* Look back at your assignment notebook. Reread the directions from the textbook or your teacher. Then ask yourself questions like these about your assignment:

   ▶ Did your teacher give you any special instructions for the assignment? What were they? Have you followed them?

   ▶ Do spelling and punctuation count? If they do, have you checked for errors?

   ▶ Does your assignment have the required number of pages or words?

   ▶ Does it have the required number of references?

   ▶ Did your teacher give you a specific format to follow? If yes, have you followed that format exactly?

   ▶ Have you met all of your teacher's requirements for the assignment?

2. *Set your work aside for a while after it is done.* Go back and check it later, after you have spent some time away from it. You may see things you missed earlier.

3. *Have a friend or family member review your work.* He or she may see something you missed. Asked your friend or family member to check for clear, understandable writing.

The Methods

There are many different ways to study and learn information. What works for one student may not work for another. However, there are basic methods almost anyone can use, adapting them for his or her own learning style and preferences.

▲ Students

1. *Read it.* Read over the information you need to know. This may include your textbook, your class lecture notes, your reading notes, study guides, review worksheets—anything you think will help you to learn and remember the information.

2. *Think about it.* Identify the major points. What are the most important events, ideas, issues, dates, people, or skills you learned in this chapter or unit?

3. *Organize it.* How did the information in your chapter or unit fit together? For example, what major categories did you study? Was the information presented in the order events happened, as in a history lesson? Were any particular skills emphasized, such as how to set up a science experiment?

   List the key points, or make an outline or chart showing the most important information. Notice important details. Think: "Major point... detail...major point...detail."

4. **Practice it.** Depending on your learning style, you may need to *see it, say it, do it,* or a combination of these.

SEE-IT SUGGESTIONS

Choose the one that works best for you. Try the others, too.

▶ **Write the information.** Make quick summary notes, a chart, or an outline. Rewrite your notes in paragraph or outline form, or just copy them over again. Design some fill-in-the-blank questions you can use to review. Put definitions in one column of a sheet of paper, and write in the vocabulary words on the other side. List the major events on a history time line.

▶ **Visualize the information.** Imagine how a historical event would have looked. Close your eyes and create an image in your mind of a math formula, or the meaning of a vocabulary word acted out. The human mind remembers pictures and images better than words.

▶ **Sketch the information.** Put it in a diagram, a chart, or an illustration. It isn't necessary to create anything elaborate or "art-like." Many students find that turning information into a picture helps to lock it into their memories.

▶ **Symbolize the information.** Make up a rhyme, a formula, a song, or a sentence. Take the first letter of each word on a list of items you need to remember, and make a word or slogan out of it. These ideas, called "mnemonic devices," really do work. Have you ever used "Every Good Bird Does Fly" as a way to remember musical notes? Have you ever sung the Alphabet Song ("A, B, C, D, E, F, G...now I know my ABC's...") to help you put things in alphabetical order?

SAY-IT IDEAS

▶ Say the information to yourself as you review it out loud.

▶ Say it to a tape recorder so you can play it back later and hear what you need to remember.

▶ Say it to a friend—a "study buddy" who listens as you share what you have learned, then asks questions to check your understanding.

DO-IT TIPS

▶ Handle the information by making models of key concepts.

▶ Move it around by using counters or other manipulatives.

▶ Hold the facts by making vocabulary or math flash cards.

▶ Master the material by making question-and-answer cards, then quizzing yourself or asking a friend or relative to do it for you.

To find out more about study habits, read:

      Homework Without Tears *by Lee Canter (New York: Harper and Row, 1987).*

      How to Help Your Child with Homework *by Marguerite C. Radencich and Jeanne Shay Schumm (Minneapolis: Free Spirit Publishing, 1988).*

      Study Skills Workout *by Susan Campbell Bartoletti and Elain Slivinski Lisandrelli (Glenview, IL: Scott, Foresman and Company, 1988).*

Managing School Work

Every student needs to learn how to keep track of his assignments. Developing a method for recording and prioritizing school work, and scheduling time to complete it, are essential to school success. Although the student is the one who must actually commit to the work plan, parents and teachers can help with ideas, suggestions, and support.

▲   Students

1. ***Use a work plan for recording your assignments and deadlines.*** You may record them by the week, month, or school quarter (usually nine weeks). Your plan can be as simple or as detailed as you need it to be. Just make sure it includes this information:

   ▶ your assignments,

   ▶ your teachers' requirements for the assignments, and

   ▶ deadlines when assignments must be completed and turned in.

   Break down large projects and activities into small steps. Schedule each step on your work plan.

   You will find sample work plans on pages 121–126. Choose one to try, or design your own. Keep trying until you find a plan that works for you.

2. ***Be kind to yourself.*** Don't spend all of your time on WORK. Balance your life with exercise, fun, and friends. Leave room for quiet times and active times. Reward yourself when you finish your work with a phone call to a friend, a great program on television, or a new tape you've been wanting to hear. Give yourself something to look forward to after study time.

3. **Prioritize your work twice.**

► FIRST, prioritize your assignments based on their deadlines. Write them on your work plan. (Find a plan you can use on page 126.) Note exactly what days you will be working on each assignment. For major projects, be sure to allow enough time for each step so you can complete it before the due date.

► SECOND, prioritize your work for your home academic time each day. Here is one way to do this:

   a. List the work you need to do.

   b. Now look at your work plan. Are any assignments due tomorrow? You must do these today. Are any assignments due the day after tomorrow, or sometime next week? You may decide that these can wait until another day. But be careful! Don't let your work pile up. If you finish the work that's due tomorrow and you have some academic time left, work on assignments that are due later.

   c. Next, number your assignments in the order of their need to get done.

   d. If there are several things you need to do by tomorrow, start with your most difficult subject or assignment.

4. **Follow your plan and revise it as necessary.** If you add more work and commitments—church, club, after-school activities—you may need to revise your work plan for that week. Remember that your school commitments come first. You may have to say "no" to other opportunities.

Teachers ▲

1. **Give your students a weekly schedule of activities and assignments.** This will help them to see and understand their responsibilities for the week. Plus it will save you time when a student is absent; instead of asking you what she missed, she can look at her schedule.

2. **Give your students a monthly calendar of projects, activities, and deadlines.** For major projects that involve several steps, you may want to note times when each step should be completed.

3. **Put your assignments in writing.** Carefully describe your requirements and the criteria you will use in grading the work. Tell your students how to do well.
   You will find sample work plans on pages 119–120. Choose one to try, or design your own.

Setting Goals

Goal setting is a planning process that gives students the opportunity to directly affect their school performance. While teachers and parents can facilitate this process, the students themselves must be the ones who choose the goal and design the plan for achieving it. They must "own" the plan if they are going to commit the time and energy to make it work.

Goals can be long-term or short-term. A long-term goal is one that takes several weeks, months, or even an entire school year to achieve. An example of a long-term goal might be "to improve my math grade from a C to a B." A short-term goal is one that only takes a couple of weeks or a month to achieve. An example of a short-term goal might be "to turn in my daily math work."

Any goal—long-term or short-term—must be reasonable and reachable in terms of the student's abilities. Remember that you want to help build successes, not perpetuate the failure cycle.

▲ Teachers, Parents and Students

Goal setting can be done by the student alone, or by the student with help from a parent or teacher. Following is an 11-step method any student can use for successful goal setting. This plan may be used as a guide to filling out the Goal Setting Plan that follows.

Eleven Steps to Successful Goal Setting

1. ***Identify a long-term goal.*** Identify *one* area of your school performance you want to improve. State this goal in a positive way. For example, instead of saying, "I will stop doing so poorly in science," say, "I will improve my science grade."

    Your goal should be *reasonable and reachable*. It should be something you know you can do and are likely to do if you make the effort.

2. ***Develop a short-term goal based on your long-term goal.*** For example, what is *one* thing you can do to improve your science grade? Think about what caused your most recent grade in science. Was it because you gave many incorrect answers on your lab quizzes? Maybe when it came time to study for your quizzes, you found that your lab notes were incomplete. Your short-term goal might be to "take complete lab notes." Notice that this goal is both *reasonable and reachable*.

    Now go one step further and include a way to measure your progress. For example, you might decide to "get at least 90 percent correct on the lab quizzes." Your complete short-term goal would be: "I will take complete lab notes so I can get at least 90 percent correct on my lab quizzes."

3. ***Break down your goal into steps.*** Not all goals will need a step-by-step plan, but some will be easier to achieve if you break them down. Then you can check off each step as you complete it.

    For example, if you want to take complete lab notes so you can improve the number correct on your lab quizzes, you might break down your goal into these steps:

a. Read the assignment in the textbook.

b. Review the directions for the lab. Conduct the experiments. Take complete notes. Diagram results.

c. Complete the lab questions from the teacher.

d. Write a summary of the conclusions of each experiment.

e. Review the textbook material, lab questions, and summaries before the Wednesday lab quiz.

4. ***Identify the benefits of your goal.*** Ask yourself, "What's good about doing this?" Recognizing the benefits of a goal is excellent motivation. If you can't think of any benefits—or if the only benefits you can think of are "to make my parents happy" or "to make my teacher happy"—then you are not likely to achieve your goal.

Your goal must be something *you* want to do. The benefits must mean something to *you.*

5. ***Identify obstacles to achieving your goal, and ways to get around the obstacles.*** If you think about things that might get in your way as you work toward your goal, you can plan ahead.

Are there people who might distract you from taking complete lab notes? Is there anything you do yourself that could keep you from reaching your goal?

Maybe you have a habit of daydreaming instead of listening to the information and directions for your science labs. If you know about it, you can do something about it. You can take notes while the teacher is talking about the labs, which will help to keep you from daydreaming. Be sure to write down all the steps in the lab setup and directions for your lab notes.

6. ***List any special materials or help you need to reach your goal.*** Maybe you are not sure about how to take complete lab notes. Ask your teacher how you can find out. Maybe your teacher can explain it to you. Maybe you can read a chapter in a book about it. Maybe your teacher can show you an example of a complete lab notebook. Maybe someone else in the class can share her way of taking notes.

7. ***Identify incentives for reaching your goal.*** How will you reward yourself when you achieve your goal? It's important to have something to look forward to—and for you to decide what this will be. Your parents or teachers can make suggestions, but the final choice should be up to you.

State your reward in a positive way. For example, say, "If I get 90 percent on my next lab quiz, I can have a friend over for pizza and a video." Don't say, "If I don't get 90 percent on my lab quiz, I can't have a friend over."

Make sure that your incentives aren't always about money or things. Try to think of activities you enjoy doing—by yourself, or with your family or friends. Let those be your incentives.

8. ***Decide on checkpoints.*** How will you check on your progress and make sure that your plan is working? Will you meet with your teachers or parents? When will you do this? Write down the dates for your checkpoints. The people who are working with you should sign and date your plan.

Students in grades 1–3 usually need frequent checkpoints; daily works best. Students in grades 4–12 usually need less frequent checkpoints; weekly to begin with, then every other week as progress is made.

9. ***Keep a copy of your goal in an obvious place.*** Write your goal on a piece of paper or an index card, then put it somewhere you will see it often. This might be on your bedroom mirror, so you can be reminded before and after school. Or it might be on the door of your locker, or inside the cover of your notebook, so you are reminded throughout the school day.

10. ***Meet to evaluate your progress.*** Meet with your teachers or parents to evaluate how your plan is working. Is it going well? If not, what might be keeping you from succeeding? Is your goal reasonable and reachable?

11. ***Revise your plan as necessary.*** If you have been consistently working on your plan and it isn't working, try to find out why. Is your goal still important to you? Is there another goal that might be more appropriate for solving the school problem? Is the incentive right for you? Remember that your plan is not made of stone. You can modify it when it isn't working. You can even throw it out and start over on a brand-new plan, if that is what you need to do to make progress.

✎ GOAL SETTING PLAN

1. What is *one* area of your school performance you really want to improve? This is your *long-term goal*. It may take you several weeks, months, or even a whole school year to accomplish this goal.

   _____

   _____

   _____

   _____

2. What is *one* thing you can do to help you reach your goal? This is your *short-term goal*. You can accomplish this goal in 2–4 weeks.

   _____

   _____

   _____

   _____

3. What steps do you need to take to reach your goal?

   _____

   _____

   _____

   _____

   _____

   _____

   _____

   _____

4. What would be good about reaching your goal?

   _____

   _____

   _____

5. What things or people might keep you from reaching your goal? These are your *obstacles*. What can you do to get around your obstacles? These are your *solutions*.

   Obstacles   Solutions

   _____   _____

   _____   _____

   _____   _____

   _____   _____

☞

6. What special materials or help do you need to reach your goal? These are your *resources.*

_____

_____

_____

_____

_____

_____

_____

7. How will you reward yourself if you reach your goal? These are your *incentives.*

_____

_____

_____

_____

8. How and when will you check on your progress? Who will help you do this—a teacher, a parent, a friend? Write down your checkpoint dates.

Checkpoint Date   Signature

_____   _____

_____   _____

_____   _____

_____   _____

_____   _____

Today's Date: _____

Sign here: _____

Have a parent, teacher, or friend sign here: _____

- -

CLIP AND POST

Write your goal below. Cut off this part of your Goal Setting Plan and
post it somewhere you will see it every day.

_____

_____

_____

_____

_____

Dealing with
Personal Issues

Self-Esteem

How would you rate your student's self-esteem? If you're not sure, watch what he does and listen to what he says. Children who constantly put themselves down, who share their work by saying, "I know it's not very good, but...," are telling you that their self-esteem is low. Children who face new experiences with confidence and positive expectations, who seem to shrug off disappointments with an "it-will-be-better-next-time" attitude, are telling you that their self-esteem is high.

Success builds self-esteem. Since the underachieving student does not experience much success, you can probably assume that his self-esteem needs shoring up. For school-age children, self-esteem is shaped at home and at school. Family attitudes, expectations (both the child's own, and others'), acceptance (or lack of acceptance) by classmates, the ability (or lack of it) to make and keep friends, and even the appropriateness (or inappropriateness) of learning activities can affect how a student feels about himself.

A safe climate—at home and at school—is essential to building self-esteem. A safe climate is one that establishes trust, respects the individual, encourages caring, and promotes the honest exchange of thoughts, ideas, and feelings.

For a student to have positive self-esteem, he must:

▶ feel accepted and unique,

▶ believe that life's consequences are the result of his own decisions and actions,

▶ develop personal values and goals and live by them,

▶ have a support system, and

▶ be able to focus on his personal strengths instead of his limitations.

Teachers and Parents ▲

TEN COMMUNICATION TIPS TO BUILD
OR RESTORE SELF-ESTEEM

1. *Have casual conversations with the student on topics that are interesting to her.* For example, you might say, "I know you like airplanes. I saw an airplane the other day that...." Or, "Remember that program we watched last week about kangaroos? I was surprised to learn that...."

2. *Ask questions that are open-ended and non-judgmental.* "What do you think...?" "How do you feel about...?" "What do you believe...?" "How do you view...?"

3. *Be an active listener.* Let the student know that you care about what he is saying. (For more about active listening, see page 45.)

4. *Communicate respect for her ideas and feelings.* Show your respect in your words and body language, including facial expression.

5. *Demonstrate interest by asking for details.* "Tell me more about...." "Can you explain what you meant by....?"

6. *Recognize accomplishments, improvements, and change.* "I noticed that you turned in all of your math assignments this week." "You really studied hard for your spelling test. That's great." "You did your homework tonight without being told. I'm proud of you."

7. *Be positive.* Look for the positive in what your student says and does. Help him to look for the positive in his own actions and behaviors. When he sees only the negative in a situation, ask, "What's good about it?" Comment whenever you see or hear good things happening.

8. *Encourage her to express her true feelings.* Allow her to make both positive and negative statements. Try not to say things like, "You shouldn't feel bad...." "Don't be so hard on yourself...."

9. *Listen patiently.* Try not to jump in too soon with your own observations and opinions. In fact, there will be times when just listening is enough.

10. *Affirm and acknowledge what the student is saying.* Do this with phrases like, "I understand...." "I think I know how you feel...." "I believe that you...."

▲ **Parents**

FOURTEEN WAYS TO BUILD YOUR CHILD'S SELF-ESTEEM

1. Encourage your child to set goals. Setting goals focuses his energy. Reaching them adds to his store of success experiences.

2. Help your child identify obstacles to success, then figure out ways to overcome them.

3. Encourage your child to take risks and challenges and stick with them until she is successful.

4. Avoid excessive protectiveness. Your child needs to be free to succeed—and to make mistakes.

5. Set up situations where your child can be successful. Provide encouragement and support, but insist that he make the effort.

6. Set reasonable performance standards with your child to assure success. If your child isn't succeeding, is it because the expectations are too high?

7. Assist your child through "no-win" situations. Some problems have solutions that result in choosing the best of the worst.

For example, your daughter has an argument with her social studies teacher about an answer she believes is correct on her essay test. The teacher, shocked by her disrespect, tells her she needs to apologize if she plans to return to class the next day. Your daughter is determined that her answer is correct and her challenge was appropriate. However, the teacher holds the power in the classroom. Your daughter needs your assistance in recognizing a "no-win" situation and learning from it.

8. Make time to talk with your child one-on-one every day. You may wish to schedule regular "office hours" with each of your children.

9. Don't compare siblings. Value each of your children for his or her individual talents and abilities.

10. When things go wrong, be sure to separate your feelings about the child from your feelings about his behavior. (In other words, separate the deed from the doer.) Clearly describe what you see or perceive, how you feel, and what needs to be done. For example, you might say something like, "I get upset when school projects are left until the last minute. You need to put your project on your work plan so it gets done step by step."

11. When things go right, describe the child's accomplishment, express your feelings of satisfaction and pleasure, and then let your child draw her own conclusions about herself. For example, you might say, "You studied for your history test and got a B! That's a whole grade higher than last time. I feel proud and happy that you worked so hard and succeeded."

12. When your child puts himself down, first acknowledge what he is saying to validate his feelings, then state your own opinion. For example, you might say, "You think that you can't do anything right. But I know that isn't true. You're a good _____. And you can _____ very well."

13. Compliment your child. Set a goal to notice from three to five positive things about your child each day. Sprinkle your compliments out over the day.

14. Love your child unconditionally.

Teachers ▲

FOURTEEN WAYS TO BUILD YOUR STUDENTS' SELF-ESTEEM

1. Watch for and recognize positive behavior.

2. Redirect and modify inappropriate and non-productive behavior.

3. Use "I"-statements to let your students know what you are thinking or feeling.

4. Communicate your standards and criteria for performance so your students understand how they can be successful.

5. Orchestrate success experiences for students who need them.

6. Provide opportunities for your students to show their special talents, interests, and passions.

7. Schedule teacher-student conferences to communicate your interest in them as individuals. Compliment them on their special qualities, talents, or abilities.

8. Encourage exploration, discovery, and safe risk taking through your classroom activities.

9. Encourage individual responsibility and decision making by letting the students manage some of the learning activities.

10. Communicate your pride in their accomplishments by posting student projects and activities on your bulletin boards.

11. Provide positive feedback on their performance, and suggest strategies for future improvement.

12. Give them time to pursue their individual interests.

13. Hold class meetings to solve problems, plan, create, and evaluate.

14. Recognize improvement.

▲ Students

EIGHT "FEEL-GOOD" TIPS

1. ***Keep a journal.*** Focus on the positives of each day or week. Write about what you learned about yourself or others; new, intriguing, or interesting ideas or thoughts from your classes; good choices and decisions you have made; ways you have improved; your plans, hopes, and dreams....

2. ***Chart your victories.*** Make a list of your accomplishments, large and small. Refer to your list when it seems as if everything is going wrong.

3. ***Be assertive.*** Let people know when their words and actions affect you. Describe how you feel, then say what you need and what you would like to see happen. For example: "I get angry when I tell you something in private, and you tell someone else. I would like you to keep what I tell you just between the two of us."

    Practice using this "assertiveness formula": "I feel _____ when _____. I would like you to _____."

4. ***Congratulate yourself.*** Recognize your own hard work. Get in the habit of telling yourself, "Great job!" Take the time to celebrate your successes.

5. ***List your strengths.*** Then list the things you want to improve about yourself. The second list isn't about things you are "bad at." Instead, it's about things you are *working on*, and that's good.

6. ***Abolish "I can't" from your vocabulary.*** "I can't" means that you don't have the capability to do something. In fact, you may be choosing not to do it. Instead, tell yourself, "I can try." Who knows—the thing you think you can't do may be an undiscovered talent.

7. ***Take control.*** You can identify alternatives and choose the one that's best for you. You can be your own problem solver and decision maker. And you can ask for help when you need it.

8. **Don't give up.** Don't let yourself down by settling for less than your best effort. Remember that you don't have to be *the* best, just *your* best.

▲ ▲ ▲ ▲

To find out more about self-esteem, read:

How to Give Your Child a Great Self-Image by Debora Phillips (New York: Random House, 1989).

100 Ways to Enhance Self-Concept in the Classroom by Jack Canfield and Harold Wells (Englewood Cliffs, NJ: Prentice-Hall, 1976).

Stick Up For Yourself! Every Kid's Guide to Personal Power and Positive Self-Esteem by Gershen Kaufman and Lev Raphael (Minneapolis: Free Spirit Publishing, 1990).

You and Your Child's Self-Esteem by James M. Harris (New York: Warner Books, 1989).

Perfectionism

How many of these characteristics describe your student?

▶ Is a poor risk-taker. Wants to be sure he will succeed or be "the best" before trying something new.

▶ Is on a self-esteem roller coaster of highs and lows. Feels great when she is first or best; feels terrible when she isn't.

▶ Tends to focus on himself. Is so concerned about his performance that he has little time to care about others.

▶ Punishes herself for not being "the best." Doesn't recognize improvement.

▶ Often quits before giving something a fair chance. If it appears that something may be difficult, or if success isn't guaranteed, he may not even try.

▶ Is less productive than her classmates. Because she overworks and over-analyzes everything, she simply gets less done.

▶ Has a hard time accepting compliments or feedback from others. Doesn't trust that others have the same high standards.

▶ Procrastinates, then blames "lack of time" for his own "lack of perfection."

▶ May have trouble getting started on activities. Fears making mistakes or not getting it right.

▶ Tends to be inflexible. Avoids new approaches or ideas; feels most confident if she can do things her usual way.

▶ Tends to be too much in control of his emotions. Does not want others to know what he is feeling. May not allow himself to really experience his feelings or openly express them, even to himself.

▶ Sets goals either rigidly high, so they may be unattainable, or unchallengingly low, so he knows he will achieve them.

▶ Believes that she "is" her grades or accomplishments. Has little sense of self separate from what she does.

▶ Holds unreasonably high standards which cause him to do his work over and over again, trying to make it even better.

▶ Doesn't value her accomplishments because she is anxiously looking toward the next goal.

Perfectionism is a problem for many underachievers. Most experts agree that perfectionists aren't born; rather, perfectionism is a learned set of behaviors and perceptions about oneself. Either a child learns the behaviors from a perfectionist family member, or develops them in response to his perception of other people's expectations. Not wanting to disappoint the significant people in his life, he believes he must be perfect.

Not all perfectionists keep striving to be perfect. Some give up from exhaustion or frustration. Some resort to angry rebellion. Some settle into mediocre levels of work which hide their earlier academic promise. And some may continue trying to be perfect until they simply stall out. These paralyzed perfectionists accomplish little, since they are so terrified of doing something wrong. Assignments don't get done and papers don't come in. "What if I don't do it right?" becomes a reason not to try at all.

The perfectionist student needs help, and both teachers and parents can provide it. Following are suggestions that have proved successful.

▲ **Teachers and Parents**

SEVEN STRATEGIES FOR HELPING THE PERFECTIONIST STUDENT

1. *Assist her in setting reasonable and reachable expectations for herself.* Help her to recognize that she has areas of greater and lesser talent and interest. For example, it is unreasonable for her to expect that she will perform equally well in all subjects. If she has high math ability, she can work toward—and probably achieve—an A in math. But she may not be able to perform at the same level in her creative writing or social studies classes if her talents and interests don't lie in these areas. Insist on adequate effort, but let her know that it's okay to get less than the best grades in those subjects where she is less able.

2. *Refrain from criticism.* These students often criticize themselves for their lack of perfection. Therefore, choose your words carefully, and be aware of your body language and facial expressions. A frown or a look of disappointment may cancel out your positive and encouraging statements.

3. ***Introduce the student to new experiences.*** It might be easier to get him involved if you set a time limit on his participation. For example, if you are a teacher assigning a project, insist that the student choose an activity completely different from what he would typically select. (Perfectionists will consistently choose the activities that have been successful for them in the past.) Say, "Next time, you can do what you want, but this time I want you to try something new." Or, if you are a parent trying to convince a reluctant daughter to attend day camp, you might say, "I'd like you to go for the first three days. Then we can decide together if you should finish out the week." Perfectionists often enjoy new activities, if you can just get them through the door.

4. ***Show that your caring is not based on the student's performance.*** Perfectionists tend to believe that they are what they do. They equate themselves with their grades, their skill on the basketball court, or their ability to win roles in school plays. Be careful not to over-celebrate success or over-analyze less than "perfect" results.

5. ***Create a safe environment.*** Make your classroom or home a place where effort is more important than winning or losing. Make it a place where the student doesn't need to fear negative consequences for being average. Let him know through your words and actions that you support him no matter what.

6. ***Focus on the student's strengths and successes.*** When she evaluates her own performance, help her to see what went right rather than "what I did wrong." Point out her accomplishments, since perfectionists tend to forget about past successes and see the future as full of opportunities to fail.

7. ***Plan incentives and rewards that do not require perfection.*** Don't tie them to straight A's or 100-percent-correct test results. Remember to emphasize appropriate levels of performance and reasonable standards.

Students ▲

FOURTEEN WAYS TO BEAT PERFECTIONISM

1. ***Use visualization.*** Mentally rehearse what you will say in a class discussion. Picture yourself doing a new activity before you begin. See yourself answering the questions on your science exam, doing a great job on your oral presentation, or turning in your research report on time. Positive visualization has worked for athletes who wanted to improve their performance on the basketball court or baseball field. It can work for you, too.

2. ***Don't start over.*** Identify *parts* of your assignment that might need revising, then go ahead and revise them. But resist the temptation to throw everything out and go back to the beginning.

3. ***Remember that there's always another time.*** When you complete a project or activity, evaluate your performance. Focus on the positive by writing some "I learned..." statements. Make a list of your accomplishments. Then— and only then—think about what might need to be "fixed" for next time. Recognize that you can and will improve.

4. ***Strive for your personal best, not "the best."*** How have *you* improved? How are *you* better today than you were last month or last year? Athletes often use this "personal best" strategy. They measure themselves against themselves, and they almost always see improvement. See and celebrate your personal successes.

5. ***Be willing to laugh at yourself.*** Think of a time when you might have laughed at a situation instead of feeling angry, guilty, anxious, or embarrassed. Stop taking yourself so seriously! Ask your friends to remind you of this whenever you need reminding.

6. ***Make a list of things you would like to try.*** Then try some of them. Take a chance on something new. When you play it too safe, you fail to discover some of your talents—and you miss out on a lot of fun. Remember to take *safe risks*. Do not risk physical, mental, or emotional harm to yourself or others.

7. ***Accept yourself.*** Learn to like who you are: a human being with strengths and limitations. You are *not* your grades or the ribbons from your track meets.

8. ***Catch yourself trying to be perfect.*** Whenever you realize that your perfectionism is showing, stop and think about it. What can you do to change your perfectionist feelings and behaviors? Maybe you can give yourself an order— "Hey, you, snap out of it!" For example, you have just finished the illustrations for your social studies report. Suddenly you notice a mistake—a line that could be drawn better, an area that looks messy. Before you start doing the whole thing over again, ask yourself, "Will anyone besides me even notice the difference?" Force yourself to say, "I'm done. This is good enough."

9. ***Get comfortable with feedback.*** Creative people want others to tell them about their work. They use that information to improve, or as sources of new ideas. Ask your teachers, parents, or trusted friends to review your work or listen to your ideas. Then ask them what they think. Learn to really listen to what they say, sort through the information they give you, and act on the advice you believe to be the most worthwhile.

10. ***Give yourself permission to be average.*** What are your strengths and interests? These are the areas in which you should strive for your personal best. In other areas, you may never do better than average. There is nothing wrong with that. In fact, you may want to write out an "Average Plan" listing those areas. Keep it to remind yourself that it's okay to be imperfect.

11. ***Say what you feel.*** Learn to communicate your feelings, whatever they may be. Share them with your family and friends. Talking about your feelings can help you to gain perspective on them. Use the "assertiveness formula": "I feel _____ when _____. I would like you to _____.""

12. ***Quit making up rules.*** Follow your teacher's guidelines for assignments, and try not to add your own. If your teacher has told you what he expects, why make more work for yourself? At home, talk to your parents about their expectations for your performance. Are you in agreement? Or are you writing in extra rules and expectations?

13. ***Get comfortable with failure.*** When something doesn't turn out the way you hoped it would, don't dismiss it as a "failure." Instead, think about what you learned from it. Pull the best out of any situation, then *move on.*

14. ***Recognize unrealistic role models.*** Television, advertisements, videos, and films are full of "perfect" people. But nobody really looks that good. Nobody is really that perfect. Being human means having flaws. And sometimes, being human means making mistakes—even big ones!

▲ ▲ ▲ ▲

To find out more about perfectionism, read:
Perfectionism: What's Bad about Being Too Good? by Miriam Adderholdt-Elliott (Minneapolis: Free Spirit Publishing, 1987).

Friends

Students typically choose their friends on the basis of common interests and experiences. However, each group also has an attitude toward school learning and achievement.

In most schools, there is at least one group with positive feelings about school. The members of this group believe that learning is fun and worthwhile, and that doing well in school has its rewards. The group's expectations are that friends will do their homework, study for tests, participate in class, and simply care about school.

Another group can best be described as "anti-school." To them, school is a sort of a prison sentence, and they are kept there against their will. This group's expectations are that friends will do little or no work, will show no enthusiasm for school, and will simply "put up with it" for as long as they must.

Your student's friends may set her achievement standards. Failing to maintain the group code of conduct may lead to rejection by the group, which your student may be unwilling to risk.

Group attitudes toward school are often very evident to parents and teachers. Keep in mind, however, that there will be times in your student's life when talking positively about school is simply not "cool." Let her behavior tell the real story about her achievement values. If she says that school is "dumb" but continues to perform well in her courses, then obviously she's still taking school seriously.

Also keep in mind that the underachiever sees herself as "not good in school." When you try to help her break the failure cycle, you are asking her to change the way she sees herself. You are also asking her to reveal herself to her classmates. They probably perceive her as a failure, or as someone who doesn't care about learning. If the student has been associating with an anti-school group, showing interest in school (and improving her performance) constitutes a big risk. She may find herself temporarily without friends—a lonely and frightening place to be.

FIVE PARENTING TIPS ON FRIENDSHIP

1. *Take an active interest in your child's friends.* Meet their parents. Ask your child what he likes about his friends—what they have in common, what they do together. Try to do this without giving the impression that you are checking up on your child.

2. *Encourage friendships that support the importance of learning.* Listen for clues in your child's conversations that reveal her friends' attitudes toward school. Casually comment on the qualities of the friends you view as most positive. Refrain from negative comments about the friends you find less suitable; you may only make them more attractive to your child.

3. *Set limits on negative friendships as soon as possible, preferably at the elementary age.* Limit special events to friends you approve of. For example, you might say something like, "How about inviting Sherrie to the zoo with us on Saturday? She's as interested in animals as you are." Your child will still see his less suitable friends at school, but you can limit the after-school hours they spend together.

4. *Encourage your child to attend summer programs, after-school clubs, or special courses on topics of interest to her.* All of these are opportunities to make new friends.

5. *Help your child stand up to peer pressure.* Equip him with strategies he can use to be assertive, both individually and within a group. Help him to develop the self-confidence to follow his own values and instincts about right and wrong, rather than the wishes of others. The ability to say "no" is essential in today's world, whether that relates to alcohol or other drugs, sexual activity, or pressures to not do "too well" in school.

FIVE TEACHING TIPS ON FRIENDSHIP

1. *Provide opportunities for students to work in groups.* Teaching strategies such as cooperative learning can bring students together with an ever-changing variety of individuals, based on your learning objectives.

2. *Change your classroom seating patterns frequently.* Give your students many chances to mix and meet.

3. *Assign partners for certain activities.* If you consistently let your students choose their own partners, this may lead to regular "couples." Instead, insist that students meet and work with other members of the class.

4. ***Pay attention to your students' strengths, limitations, and interests.*** For some activities, pair or group students based on a "blend" of talents and abilities. For others, purposely group those with like abilities and passions so they can bounce ideas off one another.

5. ***Be aware of your "anti-school" students, and work to temper their attitudes.*** You don't want their influence to result in a class epidemic. Schedule personal, private conferences with each of your negative students. Avoid class confrontations, which give them the attention they want and may make them even more attractive to some of their peers.

Students ▲

TEST YOUR FRIENDSHIPS

Have you ever really thought about your friends? For example, how did they get to be your friends? Did you choose them for any special reason? Or did they just become your friends by chance—maybe because you ride the school bus together, or live in the same neighborhood, or sit next to each other in math class?

Think about how your friendships affect your life. Do your friends help you to be your best self? Do they encourage you to do your best?

Test your friendships by completing the survey on the following page.

✎ TEST YOUR FRIENDSHIPS: A STUDENT SURVEY

Check the sentences that describe your friends.

_____   1. They encourage me to say what I think and feel.

_____   2. I feel free and comfortable telling them what is on my mind.

_____   3. I don't feel that I have to play games with them to be accepted.

_____   4. I can trust them to support me in good and bad times.

_____   5. They listen to me without criticizing me.

_____   6. They honestly tell me what they think.

_____   7. When I ask for advice, I can trust that they are thinking about what's best for me.

_____   8. I believe that our friendship is important to both of us (all of us). Nobody is always the "giver." Nobody is always the "taker."

_____   9. I can say "no" to them, and they accept it.

_____ 10. We are alike in the things we believe are important.

_____ 11. We enjoy doing many of the same things.

_____ 12. They encourage me to grow in positive ways.

_____ 13. They do not pressure me into doing things I don't feel comfortable doing.

_____ 14. I spend time with them because I choose to, not just because they want me to, or because there is no one else for me to be with.

Scoring: The more items you checked, the closer your friends come to being _special_ friends. If you checked many items, your friends must be wonderful! If you checked few items, maybe your current friends aren't really as supportive and caring as you deserve. It may be time to develop some new friendships. Read on for ideas!

SIX WAYS TO MAKE NEW FRIENDS

1. ***Join an after-school club or activity that interests you.*** Or join one that might interest you, if you give it a try.

2. ***Go to a summer camp or program that has activities you enjoy or would like to try.*** You will meet other people who like to do the same things you do.

3. ***Find a "study buddy."*** Invite someone from your class over to review for an upcoming test or work on a group project.

4. ***Do volunteer work in a place you find interesting.*** There are many places that welcome student volunteers. Ask if they have special times or hours for student volunteers, so you are sure to meet others around your age.

5. ***Join the youth program at your church or temple.*** You already have something in common with the other group members.

6. ***Take group lessons.*** Learn to downhill ski, do karate, play tennis, or paint as you meet and get to know others who share your interest.

Stress

Stress is your personal response to a person, situation, or activity. The things that cause you to feel stressed may be different from those that cause your friends to feel stressed. For example, many people fear speaking in front of a group. They perceive this situation as highly stressful. Others, however, find it exciting and stimulating to stand before a room full of people.

Stress shows up in how we feel, act, and react. At low levels, stress can improve our performance by increasing our energy and keeping us alert. At high levels, it can result in headaches, upset stomachs, exhaustion, and an inability to concentrate, learn, and remember.

You can learn to manage stress so it works for you rather than against you. Following are suggestions we can all use to manage the stress in our lives.

Teachers, Parents and Students ▲

PLAN

1. Use the ideas on pages 78–79 to help you organize your responsibilities. Knowing what you need to do and planning ahead will keep you from becoming stressed and anxious.

2. Don't overschedule yourself. Look at your monthly and weekly calendars, and balance your heavy and light work days.

3. Learn to say no to additional events and responsibilities in a high-demand week.

4. Suggest an alternate day for activities you really want to do but can't reasonably fit in during a heavy workload week.

5. Prioritize your responsibilities. Take care of the most pressing ones first; leave the fun ones for last, as a reward.

6. Get started. Often, there is more stress involved in worrying about an assignment or activity than in doing it. Putting pen to paper or nose to book can relieve much of your anxiety and stress.

7. List the situations that cause you stress. Identify what you could do to avoid them or handle them more effectively.

RELAX

1. When you feel stress building...

   ▶ Concentrate on your breathing. Control it until it becomes slow and easy.

   ▶ Relax your body. Close your eyes, start at your toes, and work your way up. Tell each part of your body to let go of tension, stress, and strain.

   ▶ Visualize a quiet, calm place. Use your imagination to take you there.

2. Leave yourself some time to do something you enjoy. Call a friend, play with a pet, or read a book for pleasure.

3. Work off your stress through exercise. Take a walk, jog around the block, or do aerobics.

4. Talk to yourself. Tell yourself that you can handle it; you are capable; you can do it.

SOCIALIZE

1. Depend on your friends and family to support you through demanding times. Talk about your frustrations and fears. Then listen to your friends and family when it's their turn to feel stressed.

2. Take time to have fun with family and friends. Too much work and worry can reduce your productivity.

▲ ▲ ▲ ▲

To find out more about stress, read:
Fighting Invisible Tigers: A Stress Management Guide for Teens by Earl Hipp (Minneapolis: Free Spirit Publishing, 1985).

Power and Control

As a classroom teacher, I remember ending some parent conferences wondering exactly who was in charge in their households. I heard stories about sons and daughters who became belligerent if a parent even tried to discipline them. I heard other tales of ten-year-olds who sabotaged home academic time. If your child sounds at all like these children, it's time to reclaim control of the situation.

Experts in the field of child rearing tend to agree that power imbalances occur when parents and teachers do not set rules and guidelines, or do not consistently enforce the ones they set. Children begin to test the limits of their power and eventually gain control of the home or classroom. Even when rules and guidelines exist and are enforced, children may test them as a way of getting attention from adults.

Although you can't expect children to admit it, they need adults to make rules and stand firm. If you feel that you are losing control or have already lost it, here are six ways to get it back.

Teachers and Parents ▲

1. Establish rules that clearly define the "do's and don'ts" of your home or classroom.

2. Deal fairly with rule breakers. At the same time, clearly communicate that you are in charge.

3. Operate from a position of strength. Use reason, but convey your seriousness. Express your concerns without resorting to personal criticism.

4. Make sure that your child understands that you disapprove of his behavior, not of him. Show and tell him that you still care about him.

5. If a problem arises, be willing to listen and compromise on a solution, but stick with the rule.

6. Keep in mind that reclaiming control isn't easy, especially if you relinquished it long ago. Your changed behavior and insistence on rules will almost certainly lead to confrontations. Just remember that you really are doing it for the good of the child. Things may be rough for a while, but in the end, your persistence will have a positive effect on her academic, social, and emotional well-being.

▲ ▲ ▲ ▲

To find out more about positive discipline, read:
How to Talk So Kids Will Listen and Listen So Kids Will Talk *by Adele Faber and Elaine Mazlish (New York: Avon, 1980).*
Loving Your Child Is Not Enough *by Nancy Samalin (New York: Viking Penguin, 1987).*

Health Issues

For some underachieving students, poor school performance may be related to health problems. Educator Lawrence J. Greene has identified several characteristics to watch for. Evidence of one or more of these may indicate a need for professional help.

▲ Teachers, Parents and Students

CHILDHOOD HEALTH ISSUES

Be alert for young children who:

▶ refuse help from parents and teachers

▶ resist sharing with others

▶ appear withdrawn or fearful

▶ are excessively fearful about separating from their parent

▶ have a hard time making friends

▶ misbehave in school

▶ have difficulty following directions and rules

▶ have a strong need to be "in charge" and control others

▶ have chronic bed-wetting problems

▶ need constant attention

▶ have problems eating and sleeping

▶ constantly complain and are dissatisfied

ADOLESCENT HEALTH ISSUES

Watch for adolescents who:

▶ have extreme mood swings

▶ have violent, angry outbursts

▶ have few friends

▶ have a high need to control people and situations

▶ can't seem to remember even non-school-related information

▶ are disorganized in their thinking

▶ undergo a sudden change in their friendships

▶ show little interest in having fun

▶ have severe depression that lasts longer than a week

▶ refuse advice, help, or constructive criticism

▶ have a high mistrust of adults

- ▶ are extremely critical
- ▶ deny, lie, or blame others for their own misbehavior
- ▶ have sudden changes in their eating or sleeping habits
- ▶ overeat
- ▶ show anorexic or bulimic characteristics
- ▶ have constant physical problems (exhaustion, headaches, etc.)
- ▶ show sudden changes in personality or behavior
- ▶ demean their own abilities and talents
- ▶ show no interest in their personal achievements
- ▶ are highly anxious or fearful
- ▶ have chronic nightmares
- ▶ abuse alcohol or other drugs
- ▶ exhibit problem behaviors such as stealing, truancy, running away from school or home, sexual promiscuity, and/or abusive actions toward others
- ▶ talk about suicide in either a joking or a serious manner
- ▶ exhibit inappropriate responses such as silliness, demands to be the center of attention, and/or unclear and jumbled communication
- ▶ are excessively rigid and judgmental in their attitudes toward others
- ▶ suddenly lose interest in their appearance or grooming
- ▶ have difficulty concentrating, even on things they found enjoyable in the past

WHAT YOU CAN DO

What should you do if you notice any of these problems in a student you know?

- ▶ **Students,** tell an adult—a teacher or parent. Do this if you notice a problem yourself, or even if you only hear about a problem from somebody else. Talk to the adult in private. Tell him or her what you have noticed or heard. *It is especially important to tell an adult if you hear (or overhear) someone talking about suicide.*

- ▶ **Parents,** start with your family doctor. He or she should be able to determine whether it's necessary or advisable to consult with other health professionals.

- ▶ **Teachers,** consult with your school nurse, counselor, or psychologist. If your school has a crisis intervention team, discuss your observations with a team member. Seek advice on the appropriate steps to take, based on your school's policies. Do not ignore the symptoms and hope they will go away. Act now.

THE
CONTRACT

Action Plan Part C: The Commitment to Action

You have learned eight characteristics of achievers and met nine underachiever "types." You have discovered how teachers and parents can be academic coaches, supporting achievement in their students.

You have conducted interviews or attended conferences about a particular student—one you may identify as an underachiever. You have completed Action Plan Part A: The Academic Profile (page 54) and Action Plan Part B: The Problem Checklist (pages 57–59).

You have reviewed various Success Boosters to assist the student with his or her school problems. You have gathered a great deal of information about him or her. With this information at hand, you're ready to take another giant step toward helping the student to become an achiever: You are ready to put it in writing.

The Commitment to Action is a contract between the student, parent(s), and teacher(s). Complete it by following the steps given below. You will find a form to use on pages 109–110.

As you complete the contract, keep these guidelines in mind:

▶ *Your student or child must be involved in completing this contract.* If you do it all yourself, the student won't have any ownership of it. Without ownership, there can be no commitment. (What if a child simply refuses to participate? See page 111 for suggestions.)

▶ Any goal specified in the contract must be *reasonable and reachable* in terms of the student's abilities.

▶ Any goal specified in the contract must be something the student *wants to achieve.* The benefits and incentives must mean something to him or her.

▶ Enough *time* must be provided for the goal to be reached. Do not expect results overnight.

▶ Remember that the most effective contracts are those that form *partnerships between home and school.* Do your best to get parents, teachers, and the student working together. If the parent or the teacher is unwilling, reluctant, or unable to support the plan, it can still be done. However, this places limitations on follow-through in the home or school. You will need to design the plan so it can be monitored, and the incentives provided, within these limitations.

Completing the Contract

STEP 1: IDENTIFY THE PROBLEM(S)

1. Review the Predicted Performance section of the Academic Profile (page 54) to determine appropriate expectations for the student.

2. Work with the student to identify his school strengths ("What am I good at?") and limitations ("What am I improving on?"). Enter these strengths and limitations on the Commitment to Action form.

3. Review the Problem Checklist (pages 57–59) to determine what you know about the cause(s) of the student's underachievement.

4. Listen to what the student has to say about the school situation.

5. Work together to identify the major problems or issues. (You may want to list these on a separate sheet of paper.)

STEP 2: CONSIDER AND SELECT SOLUTIONS

1. If the student completed a Goal Setting Plan (pages 83–84) earlier, review it now. It may help you to determine possible goals for the Commitment to Action.

2. Work together to identify *one major area the student wishes to change.* You may help by asking questions like, "Which class do you think you could improve on this quarter?"

    For example, the student may decide that she wants to improve her social studies grade, or the grades on her research papers.

    This is the *long-term goal* of the Commitment to Action. Explain that it may take several weeks, months, or even a whole school year to accomplish this goal.

    Enter the long-term goal on the Commitment to Action form. It should be stated positively—as something the student will do, not as something she will stop doing.

3. Work together to identify *one thing the student can do to work toward this goal.* You may help by asking the student, "Can you break down your long-term goal into smaller steps? Then can you pick one of those steps to work on?"

    For example, if the student decides to improve his social studies grade, one way he can do this is to begin to turn in the chapter reviews on time every week.

    This is the *short-term goal* of the Commitment to Action. The short-term goal should be something that is one cause of the student's current school problems. It should also be something that the student has a high likelihood of achieving with appropriate effort in 2–4 weeks. If you have any doubts about the short-term goal, ask yourself, "Is this an appropriate expectation for this student, based on the information in the Academic Profile?" If not, try again.

Once you and the student have agreed on a short-term goal, explain that the student can start working on it now, and needs to accomplish it in 2–4 weeks.

Enter the short-term goal on the Commitment to Action form. Like the long-term goal, it should be stated positively.

4. Work together to break down the short-term goal into individual steps or actions.

For example, if the short-term goal is to turn in the social studies chapter reviews on time, this could be broken down into the following steps:

  a. Read the chapter in the textbook.

  b. Write a list of additional questions you would like to have answered about the information in the chapter.

  c. Complete an original journal entry, imagining yourself as an individual living in the time and setting of your social studies chapter.

You may want to help the student construct a time line showing when each step needs to be completed. For example:

Weekend: Read the chapter to prepare for Monday class discussion.

Monday: Write additional questions.

Wednesday: Review chapter and class notes. Write journal entry.

Thursday: Proofread journal entry. Make revisions for the final copy to be handed in Friday.

Friday: Hand in final copy of journal entry.

STEP 3: IDENTIFY THE BENEFITS AND OBSTACLES

1. Work together to identify the benefits of achieving the short-term goal.

For example, the student might decide, "If I did the chapter reviews on time, I could do the enrichment activities instead of doing the chapter review discussion with the teacher." Other benefits might be, "I would have the chapter reviews to use to study for the test," "I wouldn't be embarrassed in front of the class because I didn't turn my work in on time," and so on.

Enter these benefits on the Commitment to Action form.

2. Work together to identify any obstacles that could keep the student from achieving the short-term goal. Brainstorm solutions, or ways to overcome them.

For example, "Forgetting to take my journal home at night is a problem. One solution might be to leave it at home until Friday, when I have to turn it in."

Enter these obstacles and solutions on the Commitment to Action form.

STEP 4: DETERMINE INCENTIVES

1. Work together to identify what will motivate the student to accomplish the short-term goal. Who will provide the incentives (rewards)? Will they be *extrinsic* or *intrinsic?*

Extrinsic rewards are payoffs for performance. They include such things as prizes, awards, presents, treats, honor rolls, special privileges, and parent or teacher praise and recognition. Intrinsic rewards, in contrast, come from inside. You do something because you enjoy it or find it personally interesting or rewarding.

Adults often use extrinsic rewards—especially those that involve money or things—to get change started in an underachieving student. This may work to begin with, but try to stay away from these as your plan progresses. You don't want to buy your student's performance. Instead, choose activities or events as incentives.

For example, the student might go sledding with a parent, or to a movie with a sibling. Parents might prepare special "gift certificates" good for "one hour playing your favorite game" or "your choice at the video store." Teachers may use free reading time, extra art projects, a trip to the media center to see a story filmstrip, or a game with a friend as incentives.

2. Decide on one or more incentives that will encourage the student to reach her goal.

    Enter these incentives on the Commitment to Action form.

STEP 5: DEVELOP A TIME LINE

1. Work together to decide how long the student will work on this plan. Determine the deadline—the date by which the student should have achieved his goal. Remember that this short-term goal should be able to be accomplished in 2–4 weeks.

    Enter the deadline on the Commitment to Action form.

2. Decide on checkpoints for reviewing how well the plan is going. Students in grades 1–3 should have daily reviews of their progress; students in grades 4–12 may have weekly checkpoints.

    Enter these checkpoint dates on the Commitment to Action form.

STEP 6: DECIDE WHAT THE ADULTS WILL DO

1. What will be the parents' responsibility for the plan? (Will a parent check over the student's journal entry before it is turned in?)

2. What will be the teacher's responsibility for the plan? (Will the teacher send home a signed card with the student on Fridays to let the parents know that the chapter review has been turned in?)

    Enter the parents' and teacher's responsibilities on the Commitment to Action form.

STEP 7: SIGN THE PLAN TO SHOW EVERYONE'S AGREEMENT

1. Make your contract official by having everyone sign it—the student, the parent(s), and the teacher(s).

2. Give everyone a copy of the contract.

STEP 8: DO IT!

1. Get the plan underway immediately.

2. Monitor the plan as agreed upon.

3. Support one another's efforts. You are in partnership with this plan. Follow through on your own responsibilities.

4. Remember the importance of recognizing and acknowledging even small efforts and improvements. Encourage the student. You may wish to keep charts or graphs to show progress on completed assignments or grades on daily work, tests, or projects.

5. Remember that it took time for the student to develop her learning habits. It's going to take time to change them. Be patient and persistent.

STEP 9: REVISE THE PLAN AS NECESSARY

1. At your checkpoints, talk about how well the plan is working.

2. If the plan isn't working, try to find out why. Work together to identify the problem. Is the goal appropriate? Is the incentive something worth working toward? What's getting in the way of the plan's success?

3. If necessary, rewrite the plan. Take into account what you learned from the first plan.

✎ THE COMMITMENT TO ACTION

1. **Strengths** (What am I good at?)

   _____

   _____

2. **Limitations** (What am I improving in?)

   _____

   _____

3. **Long-Term Goal** (Where would I like to be in nine weeks, a semester, or at the end of the school year?)

   _____

   _____

4. **Short-Term Goal** (What is one thing I will work on now that can be accomplished in 2–4 weeks?)

   _____

   _____

5. **Steps or Actions in Reaching My Goal**

   1. _____
   2. _____
   3. _____

6. **Benefits** (What's good about reaching this goal?)

   _____

   _____

7. **Obstacles and Solutions** (What could get in my way? What can I do about it?)

   Obstacles   Solutions

   _____   _____

   _____   _____

8. **Incentives** (What will I work for?)

   _____

   _____

☞

9. **Time Line and Checkpoints** (daily for students in grades 1–3, weekly for students in grades 4–12)

_____
_____
_____
_____
_____
_____

10. **Responsibilities:**

My teachers: _____
_____

My parents: _____
_____

Date of the Plan: Student Signature:

_____   _____

Teacher Signatures: Parent Signatures:

_____   _____

_____   _____

Checkpoint Date: Signature:

_____   _____

_____   _____

_____   _____

_____   _____

Summary of Progress:

_____
_____
_____
_____
_____

How to Handle Reluctant Players

What if a student fails to put forth the effort to make the Commitment to Action work? What if he or she resists or refuses to participate in change in any way?

Don't give in or give up. Instead, take a close look at the circumstances.

The student needs to own the plan. Was the problem correctly identified? Did the student assist in developing the goals? Are the steps small enough to assure his success? Is the incentive interesting to him? Does he believe that he can be successful with this plan? Have *you* been consistent in following the plan?

Keep in mind that some students relapse into past behavior patterns. For them, these are just temporary setbacks. Other students experience an even deeper fall into underachievement before the upward swing occurs. Remember, you are asking a student to change a pattern of learning and behavior that has been her identity in the past. Change is a process, not an event. It takes time.

It is most important to *stay calm*. Avoid power struggles. Remain united— parents and teachers together—in your commitment to the plan and your confidence in the student's ability to change and reach the goal.

How to Talk with Resistant Students

1. ***Give specific information on what is not being done.*** For example, "You agreed to turn in three out of five assignments each week. I have only received two this week."

2. ***Ask the student to tell you his reason for not following the agreement.*** Do not accept "I don't know" as a reason. Ask for specific information concerning the situation. For example, "What specifically happened this week that prevented you from turning in your assignments on time?"

3. ***Complete the discussion by following this problem-solving process:***

   a. Identify the problem.

   b. Generate possible solutions.

   c. Select the best solution.

   d. Put it into the plan.

Show your concern, your desire to cooperate, your interest in the student, and your confidence in her ability to make the plan work. Stay open and flexible. Listen to what she has to say. And finally, to repeat: Do not give in or give up. Persistence is worth it. The student needs your continuing help and commitment.

A Few Final Encouraging Words

Change is work. However, without your active intervention and support, your underachieving student or child may never fulfill his or her potential. Your unconditional love, careful nurturing of the student's positive self-esteem, and recognition and support of his or her individual abilities and talents are all essential to success.

Turning failure into success is never easy. But it may be the greatest investment you can make in a child's future.

▲ ▲ ▲ ▲

REMEMBER:

1. *Identify the main causes of the underachievement.*
2. *Involve the student in the planning process.*
3. *Work on one problem at a time.*
4. *Have reasonable expectations.*
5. *Provide opportunities to be successful.*
6. *Establish incentives and/or recognition for change.*
7. *Monitor progress.*
8. *Be consistent and stick with the plan. Be patient and calm.*
9. *Adjust or even throw out the plan if you have all followed it carefully and it still is not working.*
10. *Recognize improvement.*

▲ ▲ ▲ ▲

RESOURCES

☞ RATING YOUR CLASSROOM

The following list identifies which items on the Teacher Survey on page 24 support achievement, and which do not. The sections referenced in the right-hand column point you toward specific strategies that support achievement in Thirteen Positive Coaching Tips for Teachers on pages 25–28.

SURVEY ITEM	SEE:
1. Does not support achievement.	Get Them Involved, pages 25–26.
2. Supports achievement.	Get Them Involved, pages 25–26.
3. Does not support achievement.	Adjust Your Curriculum, page 27.
4. Supports achievement.	Promote Positive Self-Esteem, page 28.
5. Supports achievement.	Adjust Your Curriculum, page 27.
6. Does not support achievement.	Provide Variety, page 26.
7. Supports achievement.	Give Them Tools for Success, page 26.
8. Does not support achievement.	Focus on the Positive, page 25.
9. Supports achievement.	Focus on the Positive, page 25.
10. Supports achievement.	Focus on the Positive, page 25.
11. Supports achievement.	Keep Problems Private, page 25.
12. Supports achievement.	Keep Problems Private, page 25.
13. Supports achievement.	Make Learning Real, pages 26–27.
14. Supports achievement.	Get Them Involved, pages 25–26.
15. Supports achievement.	Get Them Involved, pages 25–26.
16. Does not support achievement.	Make Learning Appropriate, page 27.
17. Does not support achievement.	Let Them In on Your Objectives, page 28.
18. Does not support achievement.	Minimize Evaluation, page 28.
19. Supports achievement.	Build Success, page 28.
20. Supports achievement.	Promote Positive Self-Esteem, page 28.

☞ RATING YOUR HOME ENVIRONMENT

The following list identifies which items on the Parent Survey on page 33 support achievement, and which do not. The sections referenced in the right-hand column point you toward specific strategies that support achievement in Eleven Positive Coaching Tips for Parents on pages 34–37.

SURVEY ITEM	SEE:
1. Does not support achievement.	Use Moderation, page 34.
2. Supports achievement.	Be Positive, page 34.
3. Supports achievement.	Agree On and Communicate Expectations, page 34.
4. Does not support achievement.	Agree On and Communicate Expectations, page 34.
5. Does not support achievement.	Let the Learner Struggle, page 35.
6. Supports achievement.	Connect Effort with Results, page 35.
7. Supports achievement.	Use Incentives, page 36.
8. Does not support achievement.	Enforce Academic Time, pages 35–36.
9. Supports achievement.	Enforce Academic Time, pages 35–36.
10. Supports achievement.	Enforce Academic Time, pages 35–36.
11. Does not support achievement.	Share Decision Making, page 36.
12. Supports achievement.	Agree On and Communicate Expectations, page 34.
13. Supports achievement.	Communicate Clearly, pages 36–37.
14. Supports achievement.	Minimize Anxiety, page 37.
15. Supports achievement.	Build Self-Esteem, page 37.

☞ HELP FOR SCHOOL PROBLEMS

Look back at the problems you checked on the Student Self-Assessment on pages 43–44. Follow this chart to find information and ideas in this book that will help you with those problems. Look for the sections marked "Students."

Be fair to yourself. Work on one problem at a time. See Setting Goals on pages 79–82 for tips on making a plan for positive change.

IF YOU CHECKED:	YOU NEED TO WORK ON:	READ:
1.	Managing School Work	pages 78–79
2.	Managing School Work	pages 78–79
3.	Setting Goals and Developing a Value for Learning	pages 79–82 pages 67–68
4.	Stress and Managing School Work	pages 97–98 pages 78–79
5.	Stress	pages 97–98
6.	Friends	pages 96–97
7.	Identifying Appropriate Learning	pages 65–66
8.	Identifying Learning Style	pages 68–70
9.	Developing Study Habits and Managing School Work	pages 70–72, 74–78 pages 78–79
10.	Managing School Work	pages 78–79
11.	Friends	pages 96–97
12.	Perfectionism	pages 91–92
13.	Identifying Appropriate Learning	pages 65–66
14.	Perfectionism	pages 91–92
15.	Identifying Appropriate Learning	pages 65–66
16.	Managing School Work	pages 78–79
17.	Identifying Appropriate Learning	pages 65–66
18.	Self-Esteem	pages 88–89
19.	Managing School Work	pages 78–79
20.	Self-Esteem	pages 88–89
21.	Setting Goals and Developing A Value for Learning	pages 79–82 pages 67–68

☞

22.	Developing Study Habits	pages 70–72, 74–78
23.	Managing School Work	pages 78–79
24.	Identifying Learning Style	pages 68–70
25.	Managing School Work	pages 78–79
26.	Self-Esteem and Friends	pages 88–89 pages 96–97
27.	Identifying Appropriate Learning	pages 65–66
28.	Identifying Appropriate Learning	pages 65–66
29.	Developing Study Habits	pages 70–72, 74–78
30.	Developing Study Habits	pages 70–72, 74–78
31.	Stress	pages 97–98
32.	Health Issues	pages 100–101
33.	Health Issues and Self-Esteem	pages 100–101 pages 88–89
34.	Identifying Learning Style	pages 68–70

Up from Underachievement

TEACHER WORK MANAGEMENT FORM: WEEKLY SYLLABUS (SAMPLE)

Social Studies

Mrs. Thompson

WEEK OF NOVEMBER 18

November 18

Assignments:
Rough Draft for your research paper is due today.
You should have read Chapter 9 in your textbook.

Class discussion on Chapter 9, *America At The Crossroads*

Small group problem-solving activity on Kennedy's decisions during the Cuban missile crisis.

November 19

Writing Activity: Write a newspaper editorial from the point of view of a Cuban citizen during this period of history.

Assignment: Bring in an article concerning an international issue with similar political implications to the Cuban crisis.

November 20

Review the articles that were brought by classmates.

Small group activity: What current international issues could result in a similar military standoff? What comparisons do you see?

November 21

Present the conclusions of yesterday's group discussion to the class.

November 22

Assignment: Research paper is due today.

Pair with another student and summarize the key points of your paper.

TEACHER WORK MANAGEMENT FORM: MONTHLY CALENDAR (SAMPLE)

Indicate on calendar pages the major assignments or projects for your students.

NOVEMBER AMERICAN HISTORY: Mrs. Thompson

SUNDAY	MONDAY	TUESDAY	WEDNESDAY	THURSDAY	FRIDAY	SATURDAY
					1	2
3 Select the topic for the research paper	4	5	6	7 Panel Discussion Begin preparing for the exam	8	9
10 Notecards Due	11	12	13 Chapter 8 Exam	14 Outline Due	15 DISCUSSION What do we know about the Cuban Missile Crisis?	16
17	18 Chapter 9 Rough Draft Due	19 Article on international issue	20	21 Group Discussion	22 Research Paper Due	23
24	25	26 Unit Exam	27	28	29	30

Up from Underachievement

STUDENT WORK PLAN 1 (SAMPLE)

Schedule your activities for the week and block out your academic time (home study time) for each day.

	Sunday	Monday	Tuesday	Wednesday	Thursday	Friday	Saturday
3:00 ▸	Piano Practice	SOCCER	Piano Practice	SOCCER			
3:30 ▸							
4:00 ▸					Piano Practice		
4:30 ▸							
5:00 ▸							
5:30 ▸	Study Time		Study Time	Piano Practice	Study Time	Piano Practice	
6:00 ▸							
6:30 ▸	← DINNER —————————————————→
7:00 ▸		Study Time		Study Time			
7:30 ▸							
8:00 ▸							
8:30 ▸							
9:00 ▸							
9:30 ▸							
10:00 ▸	← BEDTIME —————————————————→
10:30 ▸							

STUDENT WORK PLAN 1

SUBJECTS

Schedule your activities for the week and block out your academic (home study) time for each day.

Sunday	Monday	Tuesday	Wednesday	Thursday	Friday	Saturday

STUDENT WORK PLAN 2

SUBJECTS			
Monday ASSIGNMENT REQUIREMENTS DEADLINE			
Tuesday ASSIGNMENT REQUIREMENTS DEADLINE			
Wednesday ASSIGNMENT REQUIREMENTS DEADLINE			
Thursday ASSIGNMENT REQUIREMENTS DEADLINE			
Friday ASSIGNMENT REQUIREMENTS DEADLINE			

STUDENT WORK PLAN 3

List your assignments and their requirements and deadlines on the left.
List the things you will work on TONIGHT on the right.

▶ ▶ ▶ ▶

ASSIGNMENTS ▼   HOMEWORK ▼

MONDAY

TUESDAY

WEDNESDAY

▶ ▶ ▶ ▶

STUDENT WORK PLAN 3

List your assignments and their requirements and deadlines on the left.
List the things you will work on TONIGHT on the right.

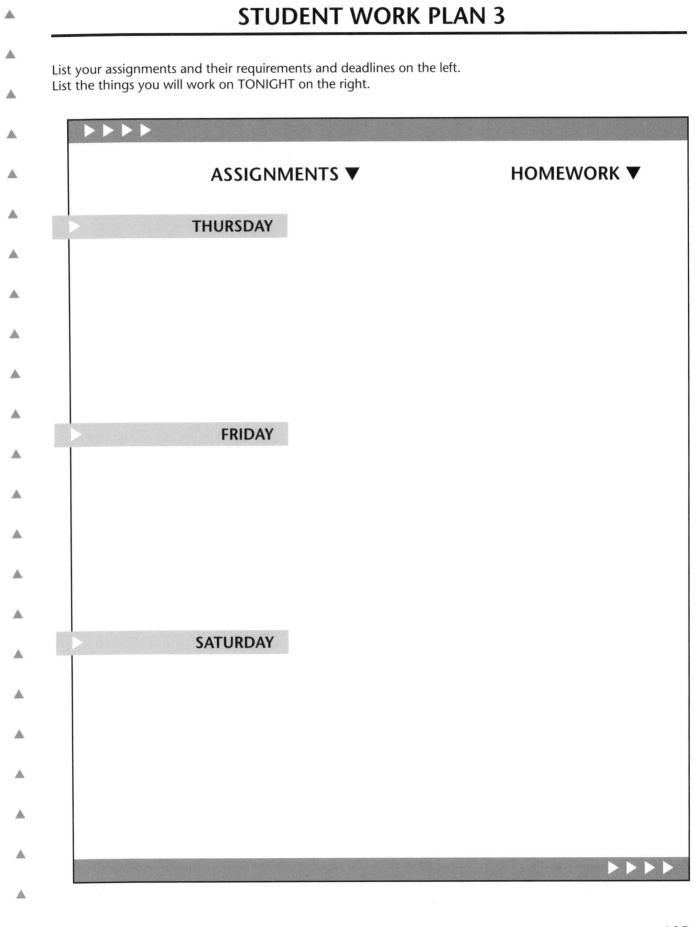

▶ ▶ ▶ ▶

ASSIGNMENTS ▼   HOMEWORK ▼

▷ THURSDAY

▷ FRIDAY

▷ SATURDAY

▶ ▶ ▶ ▶

List the assignments that you need to work on. Rank them using the key at the bottom of the page. Then do them in that order.

THINGS TO DO
T O D A Y

RANK   DATE _____   COMPLETED

☐   1 _____   ☐

☐   2 _____   ☐

☐   3 _____   ☐

☐   4 _____   ☐

☐   5 _____   ☐

☐   6 _____   ☐

☐   7 _____   ☐

☐   8 _____   ☐

☐   9 _____   ☐

☐   10 _____   ☐

☐   11 _____   ☐

☐   12 _____   ☐

RANKING CODE: A=MUST DO, B=SHOULD DO, C=WANT TO DO

REFERENCES

NOTE: These are in addition to the "find out more" references listed previously throughout the book.

Brophy, Jere, "Synthesis of Research on Strategies for Motivating Students to Learn," in *Educational Leadership* 45:2 (October 1987), pp. 40–48.

Greene, Lawrence, *Kids Who Underachieve* (New York: Simon and Schuster, 1986).

Rimm, Sylvia, *Underachievement Syndrome* (Watertown, Wisconsin: Good Apple, 1986).

Whitmore, Joanne Rand, *Giftedness, Conflict, and Underachievement* (Boston: Allyn and Bacon, 1980).

INDEX

A

Academic profile, 52-54
    form, 53-54
Acceptance
    and perfectionism, 92
    and self-esteem, 85
Achievement test scores, 52-53
Achievers, characteristics of, 1, 10-11
Action plan part A. *See* Academic profile
Action plan part B. *See* Problem checklist
Action plan part C. *See* Commitment to action
Active listening, 45, 86
Adderholdt-Elliott, Miriam, 93
Alcohol abuse, 101
Anger, 31-32
    and guilt trips, 39
Anorexia nervosa, 101
Anti-school attitude, 93, 95
Anxiety, 17, 37. *See also* Stress
Appropriate effort, defined, 64
Aptitude test scores, 52
Assertiveness, and self-esteem, 88
Assignments. See School work

B

Bartoletti, Susan Campbell, 78
Bed-wetting, 100
Blame, avoiding, 45
Bored student (underachiever profile), 18, 56
Brophy, Jere
    on guidelines for learning, 66-68
Bulimia, 101
Butler, Kathleen, 70

C

Canfield, Jack, 89
Canter, Lee, 78
Challenges
    need for, 18
    and self-esteem, 86

Change
    partnerships for, 3-4, 22
    time-line for, 4
Classroom
    decision-making, 30
    rating, 115
    and support of achievement, 23
    survey, 23, 24
    variety in, 26, 29
Classroom tasks, to break failure cycle, 62-63
Coaches, academic, 22-40
Commitment to action, 104-112
    form, 109-110
    resistance to, 111
    time-line, 107
Commitment, to studying, 36, 64, 79
Communication
    clear, 36-37
    of expectations, 22, 34
    between parents and child, 67
    and self-esteem, 85-86, 87, 88
    skills, 36-37
    of standards, 29
    between teacher and parent, 65
    between teacher and student, 67
Complacent learner (underachiever profile), 19, 56
Compliments
    and perfectionism, 89
    and self-esteem, 87, 88
Conferences
    parent-teacher, 50-51, 53
    teacher-student, 25, 87
Confidence, 10, 31
Conformist (underachiever profile), 13, 56
Consequences, of decision-making, 38
Contracts
    between teacher and student, 25
    See also Commitment to action
Control, 99
    in classroom, 30
    emotional, 90
    by parent, 38
    reestablishing, 99
    by teacher, 30

Course syllabus, 73
Criticism, of perfectionist, 90
Curriculum
    adjustments, 27
    and motivation, 63
    too-easy, 63, 65
    too-hard, 66

D

Decision-making, sharing, 30, 36, 38
Dependency, 30, 39
Depression, 100
Distracted learner (underachiever profile),
    17, 56
Drug abuse, 101

E

Eating problems, 100, 101
Effort, and results, 35
Emotional control, and perfectionism, 90
Encouragement
    of learning efforts, 22
    and self-esteem, 26
Evaluation, 28
Excuses, 16
Expectations
    appropriate, 64
    communication of, 22, 34
    inappropriate, 30
    and perfectionism, 90
    and self-esteem, 15, 85
    unreasonable, 37

F

Faber, Adele, 99
Failure
    and perfectionism, 92
    and resiliency, 10
Failure cycle
    breaking, 62-63, 93
    underachievement as, 1
Family attitude, and self-esteem, 85
Fighting Invisible Tigers (Hipp), 98
Flexibility, in teaching, 29

Forms
    academic profile, 54
    classroom survey, 24
    commitment to action, 109-110
    goal setting plan, 83-84
    learning style survey, 69
    parent survey, 33
    problem checklist, 57-59
    student self-assessment, 43-44
    student work plan, 121-126
    teacher survey, 24
    test your friendships survey, 96
Friends, 93-97
    changes in friendships, 100
    making new, 97, 100
    and self-esteem, 85
    studying with, 77, 94, 97
    testing friendships, 95-96

G

Gifted and talented students, as
    underachievers, 2-3
Goal setting plan, 83-84, 105, 117-118
Goals
    of achievers, 10
    for breaking failure cycle, 62
    in commitment to action, 104,
        105, 106
    method for setting, 80-82
    and perfectionism, 90
    school-related, 48, 58
    and self-esteem, 86
    setting, 79-84, 105, 117-118
    student vs. adult, 19
    and time-line, 62
Grades
    vs. predicted performance, 53
Greene, Lawrence
    on communication, 36
    on health issues, 100-101
Group attitudes, toward school, 93

H

Habits
    study, 47-48
    underachieving, 4, 18
Harris, James, 89
Health issues, 100-101
Help for school problems, 117-118
Hipp, Earl, 98

Home
- rating, 116
- and school, 3-4
- and support of achievement, 32

Homework. *See* Studying

Homework Without Tears (Canter), 78

How to Give Your Child a Great Self-Image (Phillips), 89

How to Help Your Child with Homework (Radencich), 78

How to Talk So Kids Will Listen (Faber), 99

How well do I play the school game? (form), 43-44

I

"I"-statements, 25, 32, 65, 87

Incentives
- determining, 106-107
- for perfectionist, 91
- use of, 36

Inflexibility, and perfectionism, 89

Interest, development of, 27

It's All in Your Mind (Butler), 70

J

Journal writing, 88

K

Kaufman, Gershen, 89

L

Learners, characteristics describing, 1

Learning
- appropriateness of, 27, 63-66, 85
- developing value of, 66-68
- differences, 15, 64
- guidelines for, 66-68
- levels of, 63-66, 85
- pleasure of, 67
- problems, 47, 56
- and real-life examples, 26-27
- styles, 68-70

Learning and Teaching Style (Butler), 70

Learning style survey, 69

Limitations, self-imposed, 20

Listening skills, 45, 86

Love, need for, 87, 112

Loving Your Child Is Not Enough (Samalin), 99

M

Mediocrity, 13

Model
- achievers, 10
- parents as, 66
- teachers as, 67

Moderation, 34

Mood swings, 100

Motivation
- and achievement, 23, 62
- and curriculum, 63
- defined, 22
- promotion and support of, 22-23

N

No-win situations, 86-87

Note-taking, 75

O

Objectives, classroom, 28

Obstacles, and self-esteem, 35, 86

100 Ways to Enhance Self-Concept in the Classroom (Canfield), 89

P

Panic, by parents, 39-40

Parent interview, 49-50

Parent survey, 32, 33, 116

Parent-teacher conferences, 50-51, 53

Parenting pitfalls, 37-40

Parents
- as academic coaches, 23, 32-40
- coaching tips for, 34-37, 116
- ideas for, 4
- as model, 66
- responsibility of, 3, 22
- steps for change, 7-8

Partnerships, for positive change, 3-4, 22

Payoffs, 38

Peer pressure, 13, 94

Perfectionism, 89-93
- characteristics of, 89-90
- methods to counter, 91-93
- and self-esteem, 89
- stress of, 14

Perfectionism (Adderholdt-Elliott), 93

Phillips, Debora, 89

Planning, and stress, 97-98

Players' prescriptives (chart), 56

Positive reinforcement
    by parents, 34
    by teachers, 25
Positive thinking, 10, 45
Power, 99
Power struggle, 12, 40
Praise, of learning efforts, 22
Pride, 10
Problem checklist, 55-59
    form, 57-59
Problems
    identifying, 105
    learning, 47, 56
    personal issues, 48, 56, 59
    problem-solving process, 26, 39,
        46, 111
    school-related, 117-118
    sleeping, 100, 101
Procrastination, and perfectionism, 14, 89
Productivity, and perfectionism, 89
Proficiency, 10
Proofreading, 76
Protectiveness, and self-esteem, 86
Punctuation, proofreading for, 76
Punishment, 30, 40

R

Radencich, Marguerite, 78
Rating your classroom, 115
Rating your home environment, 116
Rebel (underachiever profile), 12, 56
Recognition, of accomplishments, 28
Reinforcement, 63
Relaxation, and stress, 98
Resilience, 10
Respect, and self-esteem, 86
Results, and effort, 35
Rewards. *See* Incentives; Payoffs
Rimm, Sylvia
    on assistance formula, 35
    on underachievement, 30
Risk-taking
    by achievers, 10
    and perfectionism, 89
Role models, for perfectionist, 93

S

Safe environment, and perfectionism, 91
Samalin, Nancy, 99

School
    group attitudes toward, 93
    and home, 3-4
    problems, 117-118
    and relevance to real world, 12,
        26-27
School review, 42-51
School work
    balancing with fun, 78
    managing, 48, 78-84
    prioritizing, 79
    study guide for, 73
    teachers' criteria for, 73
    teachers' schedule for, 79
    work plan for, 78
See also Classroom tasks; Studying
Self-discipline, 10
Self-esteem, 85-89, 112
    and academic motivation, 23
    and acceptance, 85
    and assertiveness, 88
    and challenges, 86
    and communication, 85-86, 87, 88
    and compliments, 87, 88
    conditions for, 85
    and encouragement, 26
    and expectations, 15, 85
    and family attitude, 85
    and friendships, 85
    and goals, 86
    and obstacles, 35, 86
    and perfectionism, 89
    promotion of, 28, 37
    and protectiveness, 86
    and respect, 86
    and school failure, 62
Siblings, comparing, 87
Single-sided achiever (underachiever
    profile), 20, 56
Sleeping problems, 100, 101
Socialization, and stress, 98
Solutions, considering, 105-106
Spelling, proofreading for, 76
Standardized test scores, 52-53
Stick Up For Yourself! (Kaufman), 89
Strategy sessions, 42-59
Stress, 97-98
    defined, 97
    of distracted learner, 17
    of perfectionism, 14
    school-related, 4

Stressed learner (underachiever profile),
    14, 56
Struggling student (underachiever profile),
    15, 56
Student interview, 45-48
        questions for, 47-48
        tips for successful, 45-46
Student self-assessment, 42-44, 117-118
Student work plan, 78, 121-126
Students
        ideas for, 6
        responsibility of, 3, 16, 22
        steps for change, 8
Study guide, for reading assignments, 73
Study skills, 15, 26, 47-48, 58
Study Skills Workout (Bartoletti), 78
Studying
        breaks from, 74
        commitment to, 36, 64, 79
        developing habits, 70-78
        distractions to, 71, 72
        with friends, 77, 94, 97
        and homework policy, 73
        methods, 76-77
        monitoring, 72
        organizing, 72-74, 76-77
        schedule, 71-72
        space for, 71
        supplemental readings/projects, 74
        and telephone use, 71
        time for, 22, 35-36
        See also Classroom tasks; School
            work
Suicide, 101
Surveys. *See* Forms

T

Teacher conference, 25, 50-51, 53, 87
Teacher survey, 23, 24, 115
Teacher work management forms, 119-120
Teachers
        as academic coaches, 23-32
        coaching tips for, 25-28, 115
        ideas for, 6
        as model, 67
        responsibility of, 3, 22
        steps for change, 7
Teaching pitfalls, 29-32
Test scores, 52-53
Test your friendships survey, 96
Time, for homework, 22, 35-36

Time-line
        and commitment to action, 107
        and goals, 62
        for positive change, 4

U

Underachievement
        causes, 3, 4, 42
        as national problem, 2
Underachievers
        characteristics of, 1, 11-20
        profiles of, 11-20, 56

V

Variety, in classroom, 26, 29
Victim (underachiever profile), 16, 56
Visualization, 27, 91

W

Whitmore, Joanne Rand
        on academic motivation, 23

Y

You and Your Child's Self-Esteem (Harris),
    89

About the Author

Diane Heacox, Ed.D., has worked as a classroom teacher, as a resource teacher for gifted and talented students, and as a director of gifted education services. Her experiences include working with academically underachieving students.

She has served as a teacher on special assignment to the Minnesota Department of Education in Instructional Services, where her responsibilities included providing parent and teacher training in academic underachievement to local school districts.

Diane completed her doctorate in educational leadership at the University of St. Thomas in St. Paul, Minnesota. She is currently an assistant professor of education at the College of St. Catherine, also in St. Paul. Her work with teachers and schools continues to focus on students with differing learning needs, including females and those who are culturally and ethnically diverse.